SPIRITUAL INSIGHTS

FOR

DAILY LIVING

SPIRITUAL INSIGHTS
FOR
DAILY LIVING

A daybook of Reflections on Ancient Spiritual Truths
of Relevance for Our Contemporary Lives;
Presented in Observance of the Thirtieth Anniversary
of Spiritual Frontiers Fellowship.

Edited by
ELIZABETH W. FENSKE

Published by
SPIRITUAL FRONTIERS FELLOWSHIP
Independence, Missouri

First Edition
ISBN 0-914071-09-2

Printed in the United States of America
INDEPENDENCE PRESS
Independence, Missouri

DEDICATION

To the current members of Spiritual Frontiers
    Fellowship...
    For their dedication to Spiritual insights,
    For their willingness to be on the Frontiers
        of daily living,
    For their participation in the Fellowship of
        life.

To all who have shared our visions...
    In the past—our founders and former
        members who gave and still give of their
        time both here and in the world(s) beyond,

    In the present—all who participate in like-
        minded groups and movements and share
        in the shift of consciousness taking place
        today,

    In the future—those of future generations
        who will come to continue that which has
        been begun.

AND

To the realization of the Oneness of all expres-
    sions of life on Planet Earth and in other
    worlds.

To the unity of all people who dwell within this
    universe and other universes.

To the rule and reign of peace for this solar
    system and others, both known and
    unknown; visible and invisible.

SPIRITUAL FRONTIERS
FELLOWSHIP

Spiritual Frontiers Fellowship was founded in 1956 as an interfaith, nonprofit fellowship by a group of religious leaders and writers who had a deep concern for the rising interest in mystical and paranormal experiences. Though SFF is Christian in its origin and orientation, it has always recognized that the "numinous" mysteriously moves within all religious traditions.

The goal of SFF "is the development of spiritual unfoldment within the individual and the encouragement of new dimensions of spiritual experience...." It is precisely this goal which gives SFF its uniqueness among other organizations and movements and its very reason for existence. Though the boundaries of the soul's consciousness within each individual transcend the limits of time and space, the heritage of SFF is rooted in, but not limited to, the Judaic and Christian traditions which are rich in mystical and paranormal experiences. To understand these experiences and to help interpret them to others, both within and outside organized religious structures, is to understand Jesus' sayings: "Ye shall know the truth, and the truth shall make you free," and, "Greater works than these shall ye do."

SFF has sought to express its goal through an emphasis and exploration of the three areas of mystical prayer and meditation, spiritual healing, and survival of consciousness beyond bodily death. This means that SFF is dedicated to the expansion of consciousness which leads toward the realization of man's intrinsic spiritual nature.

Elizabeth W. Fenske
President, SFF, 1980–

CONTENTS

ACKNOWLEDGMENTS

To each of the authors for their manuscripts and their willingness to participate in this project.

To each of the artists who submitted work, and especially to Barbara Starner for coordinating the artists' submissions.

To the Office Staff in Independence for their distribution of the book, especially Ruth Rickner.

To Independence Press and their printing staff, especially Bob Lane and Claude Smoot.

To Christine Steckel for her dedicated and talented assistance in the final preparation of the manuscript.

To Paul Fenske for his many different kinds of support during the completion of this project.

To all of you...I am eternally grateful for your selfless service and the unlimited time given willingly without thought of material gain, for the growth and betterment of Spiritual Frontiers Fellowship.

FOREWORD

Dreams and visions do have a way of becoming reality when they are visualized and held in consciousness...and so it has been with this small book. It has existed for years before its publication in the ether waves and other levels of my consciousness. Now my vision is that its conscious realization will serve as an inspiration to all who open its covers and share its messages.

As long as most of us live on the earth plane, we find that our Spiritual Journey can always be enriched through the means of devotional study and spiritual insights. Thus the main purpose of this daybook is to help with our spiritual unfoldment, both inspirationally and educationally. For each day of the year we will find quotations from many different sources. Each page is basically divided into four sections. We *LISTEN* to words from various sources; we *PONDER* thoughts about their meaning; we *REMEMBER* their essence for the day, and we *RECORD* our own inspiration or images in the space left for us.

A general theme will be followed each month by the authors. It is envisioned that from this format we will explore more deeply those truths which are hidden deep within the recesses of our souls as we concentrate, together with others around the world, on the various subjects. These have been selected with the thought in mind that our sojourn on earth is experienced on both the individual and planetary level. Some areas have an importance and significance for our personal inner life and our interconnectedness with the SPIRIT behind all life; other areas call us to realize and actualize our interdependence which we share with one another for the welfare of each other and all life forms.

The messages contained within have been conveyed in the *Faith* that they may be used year after year, for spiritual truth is eternal and transcends all of time and space. It is the hope of those of us who share these pages with you that you will find in this small volume *nourishment for your soul, wisdom for your mind, and strength for your body*. It has been created through love and comes to you in love. May it be, for all of you who turn its pages and express the spiritual insights in your life each day, a friend and companion on your spiritual pilgrimage.

Elizabeth W. Fenske
3310 Baring Street
Philadelphia, PA 19104

Artist: Carol Ann Smith,
St. Paul, Minnesota

PRAYER

Prayer is an aspect of the life of each of us, though at times we may not recognize it as such. In reality, we all pray, either consciously or unconsciously, for what we concentrate on we help to bring into existence. Prayer comes from the Latin root word *precaria* and literally means request, entreat, or implore, and it often implies an approach to a deity or God by words or thoughts.

Down through the ages most humans have practiced a form of prayer life, although they may not call it by that name. Prayer is a natural function of life because we are always seeking to ally ourselves with that which will help us to transcend the day-to-day existence of our Earth life. It is the universality of prayer which justifies our belief that to pray is natural, be it spoken to a deity, God or Spirit, or merely the act of sending thought waves into the ethers of the universe. Among all religious traditions we find various forms of prayer. Even in Buddhism, which theoretically does not hold to a God per se, prayer is present. Plato says, "Every man of sense before beginning an important work will ask help of the gods."

Thus we may say that in a sense prayer is latent within every one of us. One of the problems with this innate tendency toward prayer is that we do not train ourselves in it and tend to be sporadic and undisciplined in our practice of it. When this is the case, we tend to pray only in times of urgent need and of impulse—to say nothing of the fact that we have lost a great deal of support for all the activities of life.

Prayer is that yearning of the heart to become attuned to the heart and soul of the universe and with all of life. It is as if we were in communion, and at the same moment communicating, on a telepathic level where our minds are related to the mind of the cosmos and to the minds of all those about whom we think. As we pray in a focused way, we find that our thoughts become realized, and thus prayer and telepathy are brought together.

When the unconscious mind of a person receives messages from other minds, power can be felt by the receiver. It is as if a mental radio were operating between individual persons. Our thoughts can either send forth blessings or curses into the great stream of life. In the course of a lifetime, we each pour many millions of thoughts, for good or for ill, into the moving current of human history and therefore leave our impressions on the world. Thus, it behooves us all to send forth prayerful thoughts which are for the edification of all since we are interconnected one with the other.

What we think about and pray for today is at work bringing into existence our future. These thoughts and prayers will probably come true in proportion to their intensity and the length of time they are dwelt upon. This may be what Jesus meant when he said, " . . . What you whisper in secret shall be shouted from the housetops."

This month, as we think about the meaning of prayer and seek to become more proficient in our prayer life, may we communicate in a new way with the Creative Spirit of the universe. May our spiritual life be enriched as we, with the disciples of old, raise the *request:*

> *"Lord, teach us to pray. . . . "*—Luke 11:16

ABOUT THE AUTHOR

William R. Parker, a prolific author, has been for a number of years a living example of the power of prayer through his lectures and workshops on Prayer Therapy. Dr. Parker's book, "Prayer Can Change Your Life," translated into four languages, has sold over one and a half million copies. He is a psychologist, educator, and minister who is a gentle and loving person and is well known and respected by all who come into his presence. He currently resides in Southern California.

—the Editor

To Listen

Be still and know that I am God.

—Psalm 46:10

To Ponder

Most of us lead hectic, busy lives. Thus, we need to learn to be still, to get centered. One of the best ways is to repeat a spiritual phrase over and over several times and think about it. Such a phrase might be, "God is Love." As we repeat this slowly over and over, we become still and integrated.

Prayer is a way of increasing our ability to love. As we begin our prayer time, we think of how many people we love personally. As their names and images cross our minds, we send them a blessing. We are now practicing the "presence of God." Prayer begun in this fashion, brings us closer to God. We are now ready to bring into our prayer our needs and desires.

To Remember

To lose sight of love, is to lose the ingredient that makes life meaningful.

To Record

January 2

To Listen

As a man thinketh in his heart, so is he.
—Proverbs 23:7

To Ponder

To make our prayer life more effective, we may need to change our thoughts to change our world. Look first at hate and anger. For those we are angry with, we will need to forgive, which will be in tomorrow's lesson. For today, be willing to admit that there is unresolved hostility. The anger may seem deserving, but we do not deserve the consequences.

Hate impoverishes the hater. Hold up your anger into the light of God's love and release it. This may take many times, but stay with it until you are at peace with God. The peace will overtake you and you will experience joy. You now know you have journeyed into the kingdom of God. A cleansing has taken place.

To Remember

Every challenge life presents us, is a challenge to find a way.

To Record

To Listen

All guilt is based on shame.

—W. R. Parker

To Ponder

Most therapists effectively trained know that guilt can be the most damaging of all clinical symptoms. It is so damaging because if we hold on to the guilt we will find a way to punish ourselves.

Our guilt needs to be expressed to someone, preferably one trained to help us understand and to accept forgiveness. It may seem strange, but in prayer we can look at the error, the mistake and bless it. To bless it, partially heals it. We can now grow through the experience.

When we talk about it, the shame disappears. As we move beyond guilt, we can love anew. We can give thanks. The thankful heart is always close to God.

To Remember

In him was life, and the life was the light of men.

—John 1:4

To Record

January 4

To Listen

The Father knoweth what things we have need of before we ask him.

—Matthew 6:8

To Ponder

Because there is this at-one-ment, what is missing in our life registers in our being. This is why, when we are still, things pop into our minds to remind us. This is why effective prayer changes the person who prays.

We pray to renew our sense of Oneness with God. We pray to expand our awareness, to expand our consciousness. We pray so we vibrate and pulsate to every good—health, happiness, creativity, and prosperity. In this awareness, we respond to the Holy Spirit of God. Our acceptance is an affirmative one. We deserve every good, but we must open ourselves to receive it.

To Remember

We demonstrate power by working in harmony with the indwelling Presence.

To Record

To Listen

I find letters from God dropped in the street, and everyone of them is signed by God's name.

—Walt Whitman

To Ponder

As we grow in spiritual awareness, we begin to see God in all things. All life is one. All is God.

We have a new appreciation of life. We feel one with the all. Albert Schweitzer in the African jungle came to see the Oneness and proclaimed his "Reverence for Life."

Out of seeing this and proclaiming this, we are at once more understanding and more loving. We appreciate all life and desire for it, its highest good.

To proclaim Reverence for Life makes of us a new being. We then can experience Emerson's concept of prayer: "The contemplation of Life from the highest point of view." We look past every appearance and identify with the "I AM" at the core of our being.

To Remember

Effective prayer is when we are conscious of our oneness with God.

—W. R. Parker

To Record

January 6

To Listen

Whatsoever you pray and ask for believing you shall receive them, then you shall have them.

—Matthew 21:22

To Ponder

It is clear from the above that Jesus understood the Power of Belief. Many ask but do not believe in the depths of their being that they are worthy to receive, so they frustrate their own receiving.

So, when our prayers are "not answered" it is because we are not an open channel to receive. We need to keep working to get the blocks out of the way. The biggest two blocks will be *resentment* and *guilt*.

As we give up our resentments, we come to love. As we move beyond guilt, we are no longer ashamed. All guilt is based on shame. With these out of the way we will feel worthy to receive. The channels are clear and we do not block our own good.

To Remember

As clear channels, the healing light shines in and through us.

To Record

To Listen

This is the day the Lord has made. I will rejoice and be glad in it.

—Psalm 118:24

To Ponder

Too many of us postpone living, by saying, "Someday, I'm going to Hawaii." Or, "After the children are grown, then we can go where we want." Those who talk like this seldom fulfill their dreams. In prayer time realize you have been given this new day, it's never been used, the slate is clear. Inscribe on it whatever you like.

Don't make excuses. Rather, make a decision. Fear keeps us from doing what we really want to do. Don't give into fear, it is destructive and detrimental. Affirm in your prayer, that this is the day the Lord has made and how happy you are with its unfoldment. Give thanks for this day, and every day.

To Remember

Let this day be a new beginning. There is only gladness in the newness.

To Record

January 8

To Listen

Love your neighbor as yourself.

—Matthew 5:43

To Ponder

Most of us try to love our neighbors, but very few of us know how to love and appreciate ourselves. We almost feel it is wrong to love ourselves. To love ourself is to appreciate we are a unique expression of God. We are made in His Image.

In your prayer time appreciate the fact that there is only One You. Cherish this. Be thankful. The uniqueness of you is startling. Billions and billons of people have come, and yet there is only one you. You are the center of your world. Your gratitude becomes overwhelming.

In prayer make a pledge to God that you will love the world, and yourself. You love God's world and self by giving the world what you love in yourself.

To Remember

Edna St. Vincent Millay is correct. The world stands out on either side, no wider than the heart is wide.

To Record

To Listen

For the purpose of life is to matter...to count...to stand for something...to have it make a difference you lived at all.

—Leo Rosten

To Ponder

Life is God's gift to us. What we become is our gift to God. In Prayer see youself and affirm that in spite of everything you like who you are. You can learn, you can grow, and you can change and love again and love anew. Acknowledge and accept, I've forgiven myself for not being perfect. I let others be human and do not judge. I am tolerant and forgiving.

I visualize my friends and loved ones happy and creative. I'm thankful I discovered that the most important condition for the development of love of life is for us to be with people who love life. This is communicated without words, explanations and preaching. It is expressed in gestures more than in ideas, in the tone of voice more than in words. Thank you Father.

To Remember

When you live in the now, you live in the consciousness of God.

To Record

January 10

To Listen

You possess what the rest of nature does not possess...imagination...the instrument by which you create your world.

—Neville

To Ponder

Neville maintains that imagination is the only redemptive power in the universe. If we can alter our life as we please, then in prayer use your imagination for health, prosperity, mending a relationship, and to be of service to others. It is more effective if we get into the feeling level.

Pray often using the imagination with feeling to accomplish your true desire. Be sure to see yourself receptive. Be sure you are willing and feel worthy to accept your good.

When Jesus asked the man by the pool, "wouldst thou be made whole?" he was really asking him if he was receptive right then. He was receptive and was healed instantly.

To Remember

The whole basis of healing and self-improvement is visualization.

To Record

To Listen

You are the light of the world.

—Matthew 5:14

To Ponder

Right where each of us is, no matter what experiences we are facing, is the best possible starting place to get to where we want to go. We will stop looking for or accepting excuses. There are no valid excuses.

Pray and see that we are unique creatures on this planet—unique because of awareness, because of consciousness.

We grow most in the consciousness of giving. Grow by helping illumine the path for others. When we bless and help light the way for others, we find our own way filled with light. In our giving, the awareness of our giving gives to us.

As we light the way for others, our own path is illumined. We walk in light.

To Remember

There is no failure save in giving up!

—Henry Austin

To Record

January 12

To Listen

Fear of the Lord (law) is the beginning of wisdom.

—Psalm 111:10

To Ponder

It is a law abiding universe. Jesus taught "the way" and his followers were called *the people of the way*. The *way* is the Law.

Knowing this, in prayer we know what to feel and affirm to cause life to become health, and love to become happiness. We are dealing with qualities of mind.

In prayer we are using the undifferentiated energy and it passes out into individual expression by the process of thinking—for this is the way mind acts. With our mind, we think our life and wisdom and love into form. This is the Law of Creation, our mind creates what it thinks. We know now how to make our prayers truly meaningful.

To Remember

In prayer we use our problems to come closer to God.

—Thomas Hora

To Record

To Listen

Love wasn't put in our heart to stay, love isn't love, until you give it away.

—Oscar Hammerstein

To Ponder

We have accepted a God of Love, right here within our own consciousness. We acknowledge our true identity, divested of misconceptions and misperceptions, we are God's children *now!* "The Light of the World"—we are all those with whom we share this earth. We have begun to love ourselves properly, to see in ourselves the Oneness with all other beings. We have grown in our understanding of prayer as we use positive, affirmative statements of truth to correct any false sense of God and self, and gone that further step in our quiet time of inner receptivity and listening where we can wait upon the Lord saying simply, "Spirit of God, descend upon my heart."

To Remember

As we truly give love unselfishly, we feel a presence.

To Record

To Listen

Be the inferior of no man, and of no man the superior. Remember that every man is a variation of yourself.

—Saroyan

To Ponder

No one really exists in isolation. How we choose to relate—to God, to ourselves, to others, to all Creation—will determine the quality of our daily experience. Even though we accept Love as the ideal choice, Love does not exist as an abstract; it can only be in a living relationship.

We see more and more that we human beings are essentially alike. We just feel and express ourselves differently.

To accept inferiority or superiority is to consider ourselves "special" rather than unique.

To Remember

Lord, make me an instrument of thy peace.

—St. Francis of Assisi

To Record

To Listen

Oh how great is thy goodness...for them that trust in thee before the sons of men.

—Psalm 32:49

To Ponder

Having goals is important. Striving is a positive factor—but excessive anxiety can be destructive. If you are aware of your goals and yet experience too much anxiety, try to resolve the matter by putting in writing your main goals in life. Then, ask yourself if these goals are realistic and desirable goals. Are they presumably attainable? And, most important of all, if you cannot change circumstances directly, what is there in your personality which you *can* change? What personal attitudes could be thwarting or limiting you? Be honest without being judgmental. Learn to listen for inner guidance.

To Remember

Learn to trust the inner divinity, which is the Spirit of God, and you will strive less, attain more.

To Record

January 16

To Listen

I come that you might have life, and have it abundantly.

—John 10:10

To Ponder

Are there some perfectionistic tendencies operating in your personality? Perfectionism is a futile and energetic effort to do things "perfectly." Some things need to be done that way, if possible. A column of figures should not be added up carelessly, nor do we want a surgeon to operate on us haphazardly. But "perfectionism" is a too rigid fear-ridden effort to be "perfect" or to do some things perfectly which do not really require that kind of tortured effort.

See if you flow with life, or are you too rigid? Without either praise or blame, examine your childhood relations to your parents or other authority figures. Try to determine how you were conditioned. Does it add to your happiness, or create undue tension?

Learn to turn your unacceptable feelings over to God.

To Remember

We live in a universe of love, which is also a universe of law.

To Record

To Listen

*We can never manifest a desirable physical state
while entertaining an undesirable mental state.*
—Frederick Bailes

To Ponder

Most are very aware that what we entertain
in mind influences our health, our life. In spite
of this, there are great numbers who think they
will be the exception. They are kidding themselves.

Mrs. Jones felt she had been maligned by a
cousin. She went to a healing class and when
she was asked if she needed to forgive her
cousin—she said, "No—her cousin needed to
forgive her." When she was asked if her cousin
had "stomach problems" the answer was—
"no." When asked why she was not relieved of
her symptom after visiting four physicians, her
answer was they had not found the cause. In
time, she gave up her resentment and was
healed in a week.

To Remember

*Through prayer we bring our mental state into
harmony with the physical state we want to
manifest.*

To Record

January 18

To Listen
Words are the most potent drug that mankind uses.

—Rudyard Kipling

To Ponder

Few of us truly appreciate how powerful are our thoughts and words. Thoughts are merely words unexpressed. Our words are seldom neutral—they either build or destroy.

In prayer let your words affirm the greatness and goodness of life. Speak positively, hopefully, thankfully and with joy. Above all, speak lovingly—for love is the healer. Affirm, "I release love. It does its creative work in me and through me. Now!"

By these creative acts we have turned our back on hostility and our disorders. We let them go, by refusing to give them any further energy. We have actually affirmed their opposite. We are deeply aware that our every word leaves its imprint on both brain and body.

To Remember
Death and life are in the power of the tongue.

—Solomon

To Record

To Listen

They would like to have peace of mind, but will not look within.

—J. Liebman

To Ponder

As we find peace within, we find harmony without.

As I contact the inner BEING within myself, I exhibit Divine Power in my outer world. One very specific thing that Father means is Power. So, the Power doeth the works, and the Power is within. The Kingdom is within.

We can know God as well as we can know ourselves or each other. In prayer our word so implants itself on the subconscious that it springs forth into consciousness and permeates our whole being. My own being is the infinity of all Being.

God is One Cause—I am the effect and so I am one with the Cause.

To Remember

Know thyself!

—Socrates

To Record

January 20

To Listen

For God so loved the world that he gave...

—John 3:16

To Ponder

I know fully that as I believe, I receive. In accepting, I am materializing my prayer.

My *faith* grows daily. Faith in myself, faith in others, and a belief that all things are working together for good in my life.

I know now what *hope* is. Hope is beautiful anticipation. My whole being is mobilized in this singleness of purpose, so my expectations are high.

I know *now* what love is. It is the greatest of all the attributes. It is the greatest gift. Love means loyalty. Love means self-sacrifice. Love means forgiveness. Love means caring. Those in need of help or healing, I now hold in the healing light, the white light of love, and visualize them whole. I now become quiet, and in the silence experience totally my ONENESS.

To Remember

Spirit of God descend upon my heart.

To Record

To Listen

*Be absent from the body and present with the
Lord.*

—II Corinthians 5:8

To Ponder

I am now ready for a cleansing—a getting rid
of debris that I have harbored much too long.
Anyone who at any time may have contributed
to causing disharmony within me, I bring into
consciousness, and I see them clearly and
honestly. As I visualize them, I say with feeling
and complete sincerity: *"I fully and freely
forgive you."* I see myself happy about this, and
I release them and now go free. I breathe a deep
sigh of relief. I will have no need to repeat this.
Whenever they cross my mind, I simply say, I
have dealt with this. I send them a blessing and
turn my thoughts to something else.

As we are freed of our detrimental emotions,
we are free to be healed and to become whole.
Thank you, God.

To Remember

*Acknowledge me in all thy ways, and be at
peace.*

—Proverbs 3:6

To Record

January 22

To Listen

I will give thee the desires of thy heart.
—Psalm 37:4

To Ponder

One of the highest experiences of living is to discover the unity within. The unity helps us choose that which is for our highest good.

The feeling of unity is an awareness of God, individualized within our own being, radiating out to others.

For greater unity, greater good, I need to desire one thing at a time. So, I won't be scattered—one thing at a time. One thing at a time expands consciousness, magnifies, clarifies and is more likely to be seen in its wholeness.

As we desire, we desire it warmly—with feeling. Warmth expands and so manifests more quickly, more easily, more fully. Love and joyful thanksgiving vibrate the desire into being, into expression. I am deeply grateful.

To Remember

I am harmonized by God's presence.

To Record

To Listen

For I the Lord do not change.

—Malachi 3:6

To Ponder

As I find peace within, I find harmony without. As I contact the inner being within myself, I exhibit Divine Power in my outer world.

Father means Power, and so power doeth the works, and power is within. It can't forsake me because it is within. It will never leave me—only I leave it by losing awareness of it.

I realize that I can know God as well as myself. In prayer and meditation the image (word) so implants itself in my unconscious that it springs forth into consciousness and permeates my whole being. My own being is the infinity of all being. I feel at one with the ALL.

To Remember

There are no enemies, only lessons to be learned.

To Record

To Listen

There is no outer progress without inner change.
—Joseph Murphy

To Ponder

I begin right now as never before to welcome change. As I meet change with a friendly, welcoming attitude, change can't ever make me afraid. It will be to me the joyous unfoldment of life as it was meant to be. Every change will be a new beginning. a beginning again—being born again.

As I get that beginning again feeling, I can feel secure in making changes for I accept the truth that God is really with me. God is within every change. Then, I have a center of security in the midst of changing things. The God within me doesn't change. . .even though everything about me changes.

A new beginning requires that kind of faith that says. . .."God is here!" I give thanks for new beginnings.

To Remember

None are so old as those who have outlived their enthusiasm.

—Carlyle

To Record

To Listen

We need to help people get a reverence for their own spirit.

—Ayn Rand

To Ponder

A sense of peace covers my consciousness. I focus on the law of my being—the true law of the universe—which is the law of God action. I find there is beauty, order, law, harmony that goes beyond my senses.

Peace comes as I recognize my oneness of spirit—my Oneness with God...my Oneness with the love, the life, the wisdom and substance of God.

As I contemplate the Oneness and become aware that it is the nature of my being and I become one with it—I move according to the nature of God within me.

I become still and sense the Oneness.

To Remember

The ultimate secret of power is not force, but understanding and love.

To Record

January 26

To Listen

God is our refuge and strength. . .

—Deuteronomy 33:27

To Ponder

To be still and know is a directive of spirit. I realize my true being—a law of good—a manifestation of the realization that all things work together for good for those who love God. I affirm—"the activity of God is the only power at work in my mind, heart and life." I meditate on these words—so I digest and assimilate them mentally and emotionally.

I am a channel for God's perfect action.

To Remember

A gentle tongue is a tree of life.

To Record

To Listen

There is guidance for each of us and by lowly listening we shall hear the right word.

—Emerson

To Ponder

"I am." Two amazing words. In my greater self, my I am self, I am one with the entire universe. My prayer is not to reach God, or influence Him, but to let go of reaching. I stop thinking of separation and begin thinking of Oneness.

I can be whatever I want to be and do what I want to do, if I know that I am. As I know the true reality of my being, the I am—this knowledge will make me master of myself. It enables me to live a self-transcendent life.

To Remember

I am hath sent me.

—Exodus 3:14

To Record

January 28

To Listen

Let that mind be in you which was in Christ Jesus.

—Philippians 2:5

To Ponder

I am enthusiastic about life. I am excited about changing and growing. I am turned on about the promise life holds for me. So, I release myself to the one great power and presence, and it makes everything like itself—perfect and whole.

As I give up fear and anxiety, I move in under the shelter of the Almghty. I rest in the assurance that all is well and I am well...for I am one with the Divine Flow. I visualize myself filled with the white light, and it is flowing forth to others. My grateful heart is filled to overflowing.

To Remember

Acknowledge me in all thy ways, and be at peace.

—Proverbs 3:6

To Record

To Listen

Would thou be made whole?

—John 5:6

To Ponder

I go into prayer today asking myself if I am receptive and willing to be made whole, right now. By the same token I will not question how it is to be done, and what I may expect. I am receptive to my greater good.

I am remembering with a feeling awareness that it is done unto me as I believe. Through my visualization I am believing in the reality of health. I believe in the ever-present reality of abundance of peace, serenity and joy. I am practicing the presence of God.

To Remember

We are what we choose in thought.

To Record

To Listen

In the beginning was the Word *and the* Word *was with* God *and the* Word *was* God.

—John 1:1

To Ponder

I am aware that *word* means mind, so mind creates whatever is in my experience. So, God is mind. God is the Creative Flow, the Energy. This energy is right where I am, within me and I can use it. "God, I thank you for this awareness."

I'm building my world with my words, my affirmations. My positive, creative words are opening me up to the acceptance of every good. The vitality of the universe is mine, and I am drawing upon it. I am richly blessed.

To Remember

Ask and it shall be given.

—Matthew 7:7

To Record

To Listen

Between God and man alone, there is no difference.

—Meister Eckhardt

To Ponder

I am lifted to the place where I experience the Oneness. I am now practicing the presence of God. I am in touch with the fountain of life within me.

By my positive beliefs and feelings, the universe is totally supportive. There is only good. I am immersed and surrounded by the supportive presence of God.

I am thankful for the awareness that I am involved in all life, all energy. As I experience the presence, I have passed from praying to God to the realization that I am truly one with the God within "who doeth the work."

To Remember

The purpose of life seems to be to acquaint man with himself.

—Emerson

To Record

MEDITATION

Meditation has a way of finding its place in our lives, even though we never consciously issue it an invitation. A clue to this phenomenon may be found in its definition. The root of meditation comes from the latin word *meditari*. Both *meditari* and the latin *medicari*, which means to heal, come from the Greek *mete* which means to ponder, to reflect on, to consider, to keep the mind in a state of contemplation, or to dwell in thought or private devotion on spiritual exercises. We may choose to use a classic statement to serve as a vehicle for the focusing of our attention, or we may want to be more spontaneous and free in focusing on what may choose to present itself. It is important for us to be prepared, in order that we may joyously accept the alterations in our consciousness which will come from this encounter.

Many meditators feel that through meditation the mind is reorientated to a consciousness of the wisdom which dwells within. In and through the process of meditation, we, the "knowers," can tap that state of consciousness in which we are actually capable of healing the body and the mind. There, in the silence, where the "still small voice of God" is attuned to the individual voice of our own souls, a transformation takes place in our lives. It is there that the "light of a thousand suns" illuminates the spark of Divine Light within our own being.

Proficiency in meditation can lead us to experience spiritual intimacy with the Divine and a mystical sense of *oneness*. It can serve equally well as an open door for the skeptics, the agnostics and the atheists as well as for the "believers." In meditation, figuratively speaking, we close the doors to the chambers of the outer world and go alone deep within, through the caverns of the mind, to the still point of light in which we lose our aloneness with both "the one and the many."

We have generally thought that meditation is for the inner direction of our spiritual life, and it is; however, it is also that private time when we explore what will be the outer expression of Spirit in our lives. There is power in the numbers who join together in meditation, just as there is in prayer. The Chinese tell us that we can learn more from a picture than we can from a thousand words, and so it is with the *Silence*. The work and discipline necessary to get us there become worthwhile once we experience the joy and ecstasy of *being there*.

May we this month find ourselves closer to a full expression in our daily living of the words of the Psalmist who said:

> "Let the words of my mouth and the
> meditation of my heart
> be acceptable in thy sight,
> O Lord, my rock and my redeemer."
>
> —Psalm 19:4

ABOUT THE AUTHOR

Frank C. Tribbe has long been intensely interested and involved in the art and practice of *Creative Meditation*, which is also the title of one of his writings. He is a retired Defense Department lawyer, editor of the SFF journal, Spiritual Frontiers, author of an outstandingly researched book on the Shroud of Turin, and known in parapsychological gatherings around the world. He resides in West Virginia with his wife Audre.

—the Editor

February 1

To Listen

He went out into the hills . . . and all night he continued in prayer to God. And when it was day, he called his disciples.

—Luke 6:12

To Ponder

Frequently, the Bible tells us Jesus went *apart* to "pray" and devoted long periods to prayer. But also, he had a very low opinion of ostentatious prayer—so he wouldn't have been trying to impress the disciples of his piety.

Also, one can't imagine he was briefing an all-knowing God on what had been happening—or explaining to a God of all-wisdom just what the options were. No, I suggest that he merely stated his current concern very briefly, because he was a superlative psychologist, and knew that his individual mind and his physical brain needed to be programmed with that problem, to be tuned-in for the answers.

Then, he waited in the silence for the answer. *He meditated.* I suggest that ninety-nine percent of the time, when Jesus is reported as "praying" he was actually *meditating—listening.* If you read the word "pray" as "meditate" you'll understand it better.

To Remember

The best prayer is meditation. State your concern, then wait in silence for the answer.

To Record

To Listen

Meditation 'approach' permits some use of conscious will, and yet influences mental areas usually beyond our reach in normal consciousness.
—Frank C. Tribbe

To Ponder

Meditation "approach" is an eyes-closed state of reverie while we listen to the guidance or conditioning that precedes full meditation in the silence. Guided meditation, in groups or alone, is usually more meaningful because it is focused, than is unstructured meditation. The focusing, in the "approach" stage, involves listening, accepting and following (uncritically) the suggestions of the leader—it may be your own pre-recorded suggestions that you play back; thinking about or questioning the suggestions is for the periods before or after meditation—*not* during. Meditation is *not what you think!*

Tapes of meditation guidance are available, but note *who* recommends them. Guidance voiced (probably read) by a leader usually is superior to a recording. What is your meditation goal today?—tailor the guidance accordingly.

To Remember

Use creative ingenuity and will to develop guidance—follow mentally—wait in silence for enlightenment.

To Record

February 3

To Listen

Be still and know that I am God.

—Psalm 46:10

To Ponder

The ancients were well aware of the value of silence. They knew that in the silence of meditation all knowledge could come to one—even a knowing of God. In essence, and in its perfection, meditation is a spiritual exercise, and the highest goal of every religion is to know God or to be at-one with God. This at-one-ment, or atonement, goes beyond mere reparation for wrongs or even beyond reconciliation, and in its ultimate sense involves a coming into harmony with God.

The focus of one's meditation approach can be simply the Godhead; also, it can be the man-god personage such as Jesus the Christ. While on earth, Jesus said, "seek ye the kingdom of God, and all things shall be added to you."

To Remember

Meditate on God and the kingdom of heaven. You can do no better.

To Record

To Listen

Meditation is a technique for expanding consciousness....It is a tool for learning spiritual psychology.

—John White

To Ponder

Expanded consciousness may take us "downward" into the subconscious or subliminal areas of the mind, and interpersonal communication; it may take us "upward" to the Higher Self, and to the area of celestial mind for spirit communications and oneness with God. Thus, we have opened our window on reality a bit wider than normal. This expansion is most easily and safely accomplished in meditation; sometimes, one of the side benefits of long-time meditation is that one's conscious awareness is permanently enlarged—our mental horizons are extended.

Psychology is the science dealing with the mind and mental processes, including feelings and desires. When broadened by addition of the spiritual dimensions, as happens in proper meditation, we can then deal with the *whole* person, and the God-connections.

To Remember

Meditation expands your mental horizons and adds access to spiritual dimensions.

To Record

February 5

To Listen

A meditator is one who has acquired the ability to control and to create his mental states.
                —C. Naranjo and R. E. Ornstein

To Ponder

This is a very perceptive statement—by two psychologists about a spiritual/mystical subject. Control of one's mental state is essential if one is to meditate at all. Some efforts at meditation fail because the subject does not enforce alertness upon his mind—and as a result he goes to sleep. Other efforts fail because the subject never quiets his mind—and spends the entire period *thinking.* Both problems are best overcome by the use of meditation guidance—a real effort to focus attention on the guidance keeps the mind alert and usually avoids thinking.

Meaningful guidance should be carefully selected or carefully crafted. This creative act ensures that the focus of the guidance is true, and the resulting mental state achieves the desired result.

To Remember

An alert, yet quiet, mind—and guidance that is creatively focused—results in good meditation.

To Record

To Listen

The kingdom of God is within you.

—Luke 17:21

To Ponder

The spirit part of us, the eternal soul that cannot die, is a part of God. All spirit is a part of God. You and I are God's instruments in the very realest sense, because we are an extension of God. When we sing, "Take my hands...my feet...my voice...consecrated, Lord, to Thee," we are merely acknowledging ownership and fealty that is due.

In meditation, if we dwell on these Truths and seek to be more fully aware of them in every moment of our waking lives, then the Kingdom of God will more completely find expression through us. "Prayer without ceasing" need only be continuous awareness of God's existence in us.

To Remember

Meditate on the full meaning of God's kingdom within you.

To Record

February 7

To Listen

Before they call I will answer.

—Isaiah 65:24

To Ponder

Jesus told the disciples, "I am in you and you are in me"; "I and the Father are one." They didn't understand him at all. Paul wrote of God "in whom we live and move and have our being." We are just now beginning to realize that this is a spiritual universe, and that God, as spirit, is omnipresent in everything. The great fallacy of mankind is the assumption that we are separate from each other and from God. Rather, our interconnectedness with each other, with God, with all life, is the great Truth.

So, God knows our thoughts before we speak our words, because our non-physical mind is a part of God. How can he not love us?—we are a part of Him!

To Remember

God is a part of us, and we of him. Meditate on this great truth.

To Record

To Listen

Every meditation should begin with a prayer for protection of our minds and our subtle bodies from any harmful or improper influence.

—Frank C. Tribbe

To Ponder

There are many levels and many qualities of "minds" in the spiritual realm, and only the naive or the arrogant will risk being made a fool or risk harm. Everyone is vulnerable (even without meditating): the simple act of sleeping, listening to enjoyable music, the taking of much ordinary medication, moderate illness—all may open one to susceptibility for undue influence from the spiritual realm.

Even Jesus was vulnerable!—his temptation in the desert would have been no "temptation" if he *could not* have succumbed to it. A simple but sincere prayer for protection is the easy and complete answer. A part of the old adage—"pray without ceasing"—is descriptive of the practice needed in our lives, and specifically in our meditations.

To Remember

The heavenly hosts will protect and assist throughout our lives—we need only ask.

To Record

February 9

To Listen

Whatsoever things are just...are pure...are lovely...are of good report; if there be any virtue...any praise, think on these things.

—Philippians 4:8

To Ponder

Meditation can be used for many purposes. One of the most valuable is as a technique for filling your mind with beauty, thankfulness and positivity. Modern media assumes only negativity is news; once that has gone into your mind you can't erase it—you must bury it under beauty, thankfulness and positivity.

In even five minutes of quiet, sit with eyes closed, and perhaps some classical music for background; think of the beautiful things you've seen this week—count your blessings and feel thankful—think of helping others—in the past—in the future—think of the kind words you've heard spoken recently.

Just one remembrance of positivity will do. Smile, relax and luxuriate, as you roll that one item around in your mind.

To Remember

The world's negativity mustn't sour, depress you. In meditation, bury it with beauty and positivity.

To Record

To Listen

Meditation is primariy a means to an end: enlightenment.

—John White

To Ponder

But what is enlightenment? Mr. White, in his book, *What Is Enlightenment?* says it is the sum of the answers to the perennial questions: "Who am I?—Why am I here?—Where am I going?—What is life all about?" He also says, "The *journey* is the real teaching." Reading *about* it doesn't bring enlightenment. That's one of the beauties of meditation—it starts you on that journey, and helps to keep you growing on the spiritual quest.

Knowledge, wisdom, truth, understanding, service, consideration, agape love—these are fruits that result from journeying the road to enlightenment. Focus your meditation on these various aspects of the quest for enlightenment.

To Remember

Good meditation, on a regular basis, will lead you to enlightenment.

To Record

February 11

To Listen

Mind is the builder, and the thought patterns created by the mind can serve as a hindrance, or as an aid to greater self-awareness.

—Herbert B. Puryear

To Ponder

Also, the mind-brain complex operates in many ways like a computer: For one, you can program your mind-brain, and it will follow the program. For another, you cannot erase knowledge or a behavior pattern; to effect a change, you smother the old with new knowledge or desired behavior. Meditation is the perfect tool for effecting such changes. Guidance, in the approach stage, is programming or input for your computer.

If there are patterns in your life that are a hindrance to you, you can obliterate those patterns by meditation guidance that substitutes something positive and better, making you what you should, and want, to be. Mind controls the body—it builds for ill or for good.

To Remember

Program your mind-brain for good, and watch your life blossom.

To Record

To Listen

In the life of every seeker-meditator...there comes a time when he...becomes aware...of an actual transcendental Presence and Power.

—Joel S. Goldsmith

To Ponder

Persons who long for a mystical experience would be well advised to take up creative meditation as a serious pursuit. Regular meditation, which is focused primarily on enhancement of the world and one's life in it, will certainly, in time, result in the "transcendental Presence and Power" that Goldsmith writes about. Neither prayer, piety nor good works are as certain to bring the mystical event. Not that mysticism can be earned—rather, one attunes oneself to the celestial, even to the Infinite, by such meditation.

When so attuned, one is in the environment of transcendental Presence and Power. This is where mystical events happen—the seeker-meditator is in the right place. What has always been possible, becomes much more probable.

To Remember

A true mystical experience is more likely to come to a creative seeker-meditator.

To Record

To Listen

In meditation, the consciousness becomes inevitably like that on which we have 'gazed'.

—M. V. Dunlop

To Ponder

On what have you "gazed"? On what have you put your attention, given your time and supported with your mental power? If we have gazed upon the beautiful, the profound, the important, the valuable, then in meditation (the author tells us) our consciousness will become like it.

One who leads a shallow and relatively useless life cannot expect meditation to work wonders for him, without more. Meditation can be the first step, and can be the tool with which he reevaluates his life; thereafter, it might also be the tool for guiding the meditator into a useful life, where he may have the perspicacity to gaze on the beautiful and the valuable in the world. To what do we give our time and our money?

To Remember

Look up! Fix your gaze on important things. Meditate, and your consciousness will profit therefrom.

To Record

To Listen

Most of us pray that God will do something to us or for us; God wants to do something in us and through us.

—Grace Adolphsen Brame

To Ponder

I am sure that Mrs. Brame is exactly right—though not necessarily unique. Lao Russell, inspired by her late husband, Walter, wrote a book titled, *God Will Work With You, but Not For You.* Mrs. Brame has perhaps stated the thought better. The thought is highly provocative. It behooves us to phrase our prayers and the guidance in our meditations more carefully.

It is a time-honored but much ignored truism that we should not try to tell God how to fulfill our needs—he knows best! Rarely does God take the shortcut and lay the prize in our laps. If we will work in his vineyard, he will guide our hands—and the harvest will be greater than we could have imagined.

To Remember

Meditate to learn God's will in your life; seek to be his hands.

To Record

February 15

To Listen

The thing I greatly feared has come upon me.
—Job 3:25

To Ponder

What we concentrate upon, we attract to us. Fear is one of the strongest emotions in the human arsenal. Embrace it sparingly; forget your fears most of the time. Above all, don't worry about your fears; just do what you can to preclude their fulfillment, then forget them.

In meditation, affirm the positive and the good that is the opposite of what you fear. Even if you can't believe or accept anything that good, say it anyway! Repeat the affirmation over and over, programming it into your unconscious mind during the approach phase of your guided meditation. Obliterate the negativity and your fears with the repetition of your positive affirmation.

To Remember

Fill not only your meditation but all waking moments possible with positive affirmations.

To Record

To Listen

The Lord was not in the wind...in the earth-quake...in the fire; and after the fire a still, small voice. And it was so.

—I Kings 19:12–13

To Ponder

The still, small voice is the voice that comes in the meditation silence—it may be the voice of God. Ask that any answer received in medita-tion be "of God." The apostle wrote, "Test the spirits to see whether they are of God" (I John 4:1). Later, ask yourself, "does the answer guide me into a more loving, serving life?" If you follow the advice, "do you feel a sense of fulfill-ment of the best within you?" If your answer is, "yes," probably the guidance was "of God."

A lifetime of meditation may never bring a *voice* into your silences. Maybe a clear "knowing," "thought" or "idea" is sensed but not expressed in words—these may be equally important and may indeed be "of God."

To Remember

Every meditation guidance may be "of God." If a VOICE does come, you are BLESSED.

To Record

February 17

To Listen

Meditation is a simple process that will encourage you to be the person you were meant to be.

—Roy Eugene Davis

To Ponder

Do you know what you were meant to be? Do you want to know? If you knew, would you have the ambition and drive to get there? Many persons are satisfied with much less than they could be—how about you?

Meditation, creatively and regularly pursued, can be the technique by which you can learn what you were meant to be. Once the goal is established, meditation becomes the channel through which your Higher Self will inspire and encourage you to go for that goal; also it will open doors for you, and even gently push you through them!

Yes, a simple process: still the body; still the mind while keeping it alert; focus the mind, and wait in the silence—a simple process.

To Remember

You can know what you were meant to be—and you can get there. Meditate.

To Record

To Listen

Means for growth offered in our churches are worship, prayer, study, and service....None is adequate without the touchstone of an inner awareness.

—Fay Conlee Oliver

To Ponder

A touchstone is a test or criterion for determining quality or genuineness. We can only measure quality or genuineness of worship, prayer, religious study, and service by the reaction of our own inner awareness—not the opinion of another. But how do we get in touch with this inner awareness?—how do we hone it to keen sensibility?—how do we get reliable feedback from our inner awareness? Through meditation, that's how.

Years of regular meditation give easy and instant access to our inner awareness. But without that background, what can we do? Program our unconscious, our mind, in guided meditation, and listen for answers in the silence, Our religious life is only as good for us as our inner awareness tells us it is.

To Remember

Go within to evaluate your religious life.

To Record

To Listen

Accomplishments in meditation can include spiritual growth, development of channels to the higher self, sending healing to others, and wooing of the Christ consciousness.

—Frank C. Tribbe

To Ponder

There's nothing wrong with using meditation to bring deep relaxation and to overcome stress. Those results will come automatically with meditation, but it's a shame to stop there!— meditation can do so much more for you.

Either you, or your group leader, can easily structure the "approach" phase of guided meditations so that the period in the silence can be focused—then enlightenment of many sorts can come to you. What do you want, specifically?— A mystical dimension in your life?—A closer relationship with the Christ, or with the Jesus entity?—Insight and wisdom in certain areas?— To be more loving and helpful?—To achieve self-healing, or to heal others? During "approach," focus on what you want, then wait for it.

To Remember

Enlightenment through meditation is unlimited. Create meditations that bring what you want.

To Record

To Listen
Let go, and let God.

—Anonymous

To Ponder
A problem is never solved by clutching it to your bosom; try to resolve it promptly and then forget it. Worrying about unresolved problems reinforces the negative situations, and the side-effect is like a headache from butting your head against a wall.

Handle problems you seemingly can't solve, this way: take a plastic margarine cup and cover; clean them, and label the cover, *"God's Bowl."* *Briefly,* write out the unresolved problem on paper, and put in the bowl.

In meditation, tell God you've put this problem in His bowl, and that *you've let go of it.* Each time you think of the problem, push it out of your mind, telling yourself, "It's in God's Bowl." In meditation or dreams a solution may be given you.

To Remember
Problems go away or solve themselves when put in God's Bowl. Update the bowl monthly.

To Record

February 21

To Listen

The common core of all meditation experiences is an altered state of consciousness that leads to a diminishing of ego.

—John White

To Ponder

The above statement assumes that all of us have overgrown egos that need to be diminished in size. Some eastern religions seem to teach the subservience of ego and ultimate extinction of it; such a theology is neither compatible with the Judeo-Christian view of mankind, nor is it consistent with the human nature which God created in us. Ego is not evil, unless through exercise of our free-will, we make it so.

What does seem error in modern man is the bent toward self-centeredness and self-gratification. These philosophies of life will result in inordinately large egos, out of balance with the rest of our being. In meditation, ask that the selfless aspects of your nature grow to balance the selfishness of your ego.

To Remember

Balance of the ego with other aspects of the human nature is possible in meditation.

To Record

To Listen

Maintain an alert unthinkingness throughout your meditation.... Affirm: 'I am attuned to the Christ Mind'.

—Marjorie Russell

To Ponder

In meditation—both in meditation approach and in the silence—the mind must be alert, *but not thinking.* An "alert unthinkingness" is the true meditation stance. During meditation approach your mind should listen and accept the guidance, but not think about it. During meditation in the silence, one should listen and *feel* with expectation.

How does one achieve an "alert unthinkingness"? There are several ways—one of the easiest is by use of a mantra—westerners might more naturally call it an affirmation. Mrs. Russell suggests you affirm silently: "I am attuned to the Christ Mind"—or you can make up your own. Repeat it a half-dozen times in the silence, and then listen. If you start to *think,* repeat the affirmation.

To Remember

In meditation, if you start to think, repeat your affirmation.

To Record

February 23

To Listen

*I will meditate on thy precepts, and fix my eyes
on thy ways.*

—Psalm 119:15

To Ponder

God's precepts are his commandments—his
rules of moral conduct. Meditate upon one of
them to receive insight of application to one's
life. Insight will indicate how we may be violating that rule, and how we might change attitude
or conduct to come into harmony with it. List
the Commandments and all other rules of God
you can. Then, one at a time, meditate on each—
don't skip one, even though you think you have
never violated it. Insights may be surprising.

If we fix our "eyes" on God's ways, we are
more apt to use them as patterns for our own
lives. How can we know God's ways? In meditation, ask what would be God's way in every
situation of ours?

To Remember

*Meditate on God's rules; learn his ways to use as
your guide.*

To Record

To Listen

Three-fourths of our patients are passing on the sickness of their minds and their souls to their bodies.

—The Mayo Clinic

To Ponder

Be careful of the beliefs you hold and the thoughts you *repeatedly* think. In *Proverbs* (6:27) the writer asks, "Can a man take fire unto his bosom, and his clothes not be burned?" More specifically, we can ask: can a man take fears, doubts, hatreds, resentments, worries into his mind, and his body be unaffected?

Use your meditation period to "purify" your mind. During the day, make note of your negative thoughts—especially those that are repeating and are non-productive. In meditation, smother that negativity with affirmations of a positive and constructive tone, using the opposites of your previous negative thoughts. Don't be afraid of becoming a "Pollyanna." Positive thinking can't harm you!

To Remember

Optimism and positive thinking are good for your health!

To Record

February 25

I will meditate on thy wondrous works.
                                    —Psalm 119:27

To Ponder

Yes, the works of God are truly wondrous, and they make an excellent focus for our meditations. What grandeur of nature appeals most to you?—the purple mountain majesties?—the foaming surf of the oceanside?—amber fields of grain on the fruited plain?—alabaster cities seen from an airplane window?—spacious skies heaped with billowing clouds painted with sunset rose?—the forest glades colored by an autumn frost?—the planets and stars of a thousand galaxies? Pick the facet of God's wondrous works that appeals to you and make it the focus of a meditation.

Tranquility is sure to abound in such a meditation, and its natural climax is a feeling of praise when one's thoughts of God bring the conclusion, "How great thou art!"

To Remember

Tranquility and praise come out of meditations focused on God's wondrous works.

To Record

To Listen

*Learn the art of continuing ourselves before it is
too late.... Discover a source of strength as wonderful as it is accessible.*

—Bradford Smith

To Ponder

Most of us know our own faults and our
shortcomings, but it's uncomfortable to think
about them, so we don't seriously consider
changing. But we can! One of the easiest and
most effective ways to change ourselves is
through meditation—creative meditation by
self-created guidance—and we can do it privately.

Make a list of those traits and personal
practices that are causing problems—ones you
would be willing to do without. Opposite each,
describe the positive conduct on your part
which would eliminate the undesirable item.
(For we know that in meditation, as in prayer,
we must not give power to a negative, by our
thought or word.) *One at a time*, "program"
your mind with those items of positive conduct
in the "approach."

To Remember

*Confront yourself the painless way—in medi-
tation—to correct your flaws.*

To Record

To Listen

Concentration entirely on my inward self. . . . Not taking the trouble to know you. . . is a much greater loss to me. . . than to you.

—Ardis Whitman

To Ponder

Self-centeredness is more prevalent and more likely today than in ages past. Unfortunately, many New-Age disciplines and leaders stress self-development and largely ignore service to others. The great Nazarene said, "love your neighbor as yourself." Also, the absence—for so many—of a nurturing family situation, leads toward an exclusively inward focusing. Loneliness begets self-centeredness.

This risk of loss, in "not taking the trouble to know you," can most easily be overcome in meditation—*guided* meditation. In creating the guidance, the approach, consider how you can bring them into your life: relatives, neighbors, church members, the sick, business associates. In the meditation guidance, tell yourself whom you want to know better—and truly want it.

To Remember

In silence, ways to know others better and the will to do so may come.

To Record

To Listen

Higher meditation...occurs....The spiritual center of gravity...shifts....The inner life becomes the definite reality...life of the world but a pale reflection.

— Christmas Humphries

To Ponder

The inner life is the true Reality. Yes. But the author is referring to quality, not quantity. He is not advocating an ascetic life, a retreat from activity in the world. Excessive meditation is not recommended; fifteen to twenty-five minutes each meditation, and once or twice a day gives all a person requires. But, with regularity, meditation can become the "definite Reality" the author has in mind—it can become so valuable that life in the world is a "pale reflection" by comparison.

However, comparisons are often misleading. Life in the world should not be disdained. When focus of the inner life, through meditation, is set on making life in the world more valuable, it will be so. It is the total life that one must judge.

To Remember

The focus of meditation should be to enhance one's life in the world.

To Record

February 29

To Listen

We meditate to find. . . something of ourselves we once. . . unknowingly had and have lost, without knowing what it was. . . or when we lost it.
—Lawrence LeShan

To Ponder

Does your life seem empty, inadequate, unfulfilling, sad? Is something seemingly missing that you feel you must have previously had, at a time when life was happier for you? Is there a way to identify that missing something, and perhaps a way to get it back into your life? Yes. And the way is meditation.

Meditation has many practical and valuable uses, and one of them is to identify a problem that is too vaguely felt to be consciously named. Through your meditation approach, ask that the unknown missing ingredient be identified. After that has happened, you can ask for solutions which will put that ingredient back into your life. Be persistent and patient, for there may be several possible solutions from which to choose.

To Remember

If your life is not fully satisfying, meditation may solve the problem.

To Record

SELF HEALING

All healing is in reality Self Healing. Because we each create our own realities and manifest in our lives situations which need to be held in the healing light and love, we are therefore called to participate in bringing into manifestation the healing process. The word healing comes from the Old English root word *hal* and literally means to make whole or sound or healthy.

We accept the fact that healing comes to each of us through many different healing modalities. We are all familiar with and very grateful for physical healings of the body through the medical model. Some of us have experienced a relief of mental and emotional suffering through the psychiatric and psychological models. The religious model of sacramental and spiritual healing combines the curative potential of words and touch and often involves a flow of energy emanating from the endless supply within the universe. This flow of energy becomes focused within the healee to bring about a change for a greater degree of wholeness.

It is very difficult to make clearcut distinctions between various forms of healing. Often we do not know exactly what caused the healing to occur, just as we do not know exactly what caused the distress. Both the symptoms and the resources for healing lie deeply buried within our being. In an often strange and mysterious way the forces of illness and health, of the ego and the soul, and the roles of the healer and healee co-exist within the unconscious of each of us. Faust said it with the words: "Two souls, alas, dwell in my breast apart." We must always be about exploring various expressions of healing, both the older expressions of yesteryear and the newer expressions of today and tomorrow. Often we find that the new is but an expression of the old at its inception.

The Swiss psychoanalyst C. G. Jung explained through his work that no time or space exists in the unconscious realm of the psyche where both inner and outer events are connected. An application of these principles points out that healing comes both from within the psyche and from the universe with which we are interconnected at a deep level. The example is often used of a spring bubbling up into a lake. The spring is both within and outside the lake; a blockage of the spring would be analogous to our inability to be healed. The blockage to healing prevents the free flow of wholeness and love from manifesting in our lives.

As we approach the area of healing this month, may we consciously look at that which is within in order that we might change that which we reflect. Often that which is in our past tends to cloud and distort that which we outwardly exemplify in our daily living. May we come expecting and asking for healing, being receptive to that which is our birthright, and giving thanks for that which has happened and is happening in our life.

In order to appreciate fully the wholeness of body, mind, and spirit in our lives, we must heed and experience the admonition:

> "Physician, Heal Thyself."—Luke 4:23

ABOUT THE AUTHOR

Lawrence W. Althouse is known across the country and abroad as a pastor, a healer, a travel leader and an author. As a minister and healer, he has conducted weekly healing services. Among his books is Rediscovering the Gift of Healing, and for more than twenty years he has written weekly syndicated columns on religion and travel. He is a Past President of SFF and resides with his wife Valere in Dallas, Texas.

—the Editor

To Listen

When Jesus saw him and knew that he had been lying there a long time, he said to him, "Do you want to be healed?"

—John 5:6

To Ponder

It seems a strange question to ask a man who had lain by the Pool of Bathzatha for 38 years, waiting for an angel to heal him. "Sir," answered the man, "I have no man to put me into the pool when the water is troubled..." But Jesus was giving him a choice: between continuing to lie there and wallow in self-pity or accepting the wholeness that was offered him.

Dr. Arnold Hutschnecker says it is difficult for young doctors to realize that some people don't want to get well. They say they want to be healed and they think they do, but it is not their dominant desire.

To Remember

Prayer that is not dominant desire is too weak to achieve anything.

—Harry Emerson Fosdick

To Record

March 2

To Listen

One thing you still lack. Sell all that you have and distribute to the poor, and you will have treasure in heaven.

—Luke 18:22

To Ponder

Hearing these words, the rich young ruler "became sad, for he was very rich." He had told Jesus that "treasure in heaven" was his heart's desire, but it was soon evident that he wanted something more than eternal life.

So it may be with healing. It seems we want it more than anything in the world—until someone points out that there is still something we must give up: perhaps an attitude, a grudge, an unhealthy habit or practice, maybe even the power we gain over others with our sickness. Faced with the choice of gaining wholeness and giving up our security blanket, some people sadly choose to hold on to the latter.

When seeking healing, let us first ask ourselves: is there one thing I "still lack"?

To Remember

A merchant...on finding one pearl of great value, went and sold all that he had and bought it.

—Matthew 13:46

To Record

To Listen

And Jesus said to him, "What do you want me to do for you?" And the blind man said... "Master, let me receive my sight."

—Mark 10:51

To Ponder

Jesus didn't ask the blind Bartimaeus what he *wished*; he asked what he *wanted*. Bartimaeus's "Jesus, Son of David, have mercy on me!" was too vague. And so are many of our prayers—because they are wishes instead of expressions of will.

A New England school master, Dr. Finney, was heard to pray: "And thou knowest, O Lord, that in these matters I am not accustomed to be denied." Audacious words, perhaps, but when we live lives close to God we can afford to pray with the assurance that God wants us whole—even more than we do.

The Great Physician challenges us, no less than Bartimaeus, to pray boldly and clearly for guidance in answering the question: "What do you want me to do for you?"

To Remember

Ask, and it will be given you; seek, and you will find; knock, and it will be opened to you.

—Matthew 7:7

To Record

March 4

The prayer of faith will save the sick man, and the Lord will raise him up.

—James 5:15

To Ponder

The Rev. Bruce Larson tells of arriving at a religious conference several years ago with a number of flu symptoms. Within an hour's time, upon learning he was ill, six different people arrived at his room to minister to him. The first person anointed him with oil. A second person knelt and offered a prayer. The third, a doctor, took his pulse and gave him some aspirin. Another person brought a tray of food, and still another came and chatted with him briefly. The sixth person gave him a massage and sang some hymns in Finnish.

Larson comments: "I was healed within the hour. I don't know which of these people was the channel of God's healing, but I suspect they were all used."

To Remember

I dressed his wounds and God healed him.

—Ambrose Paré

To Record

To Listen

I ask you, is it lawful on the sabbath to do good or to do harm, to save life or to destroy it?

—Luke 6:9

To Ponder

Question: In which of his many, many healings did Jesus first question as to whether it was God's will?

Answer: None of them!

Jesus never questioned if it was God's will to heal any of those who came to him for healing. Why? Obviously, because he worked on the assumption that God wills for all of us to be whole. If, as some people assume, God wants some of us to be well and others to be ill, then Jesus would have healed some supplicants, but not others.

Thus, in seeking healing, we can pray with assurance: "Thy will be done."

To Remember

We pray, not in order to alter his will, but to bring ourselves in accordance with it.

—Emily Gardner Neal

To Record

March 6

To Listen

And demons also came out of many, crying, "You are the Son of God!" But he rebuked them.

—Luke 4:41

To Ponder

One of the strange ideas with which some people respond to illness is that it may sometimes be regarded as a "friend" sent to teach us something necessary for our own good. This was hardly the way Jesus viewed it in the New Testament. He never told anyone that God had sent them sickness so that they might "grow"! The demons Jesus cast out were the enemies of God, not his little helpers. Two German scholars, Klaus Seybold and Ulrich Müller, have characterized the view of the New Testament: "God stands against sickness, not with it!...Sickness contradicts the salvation will of the creator God, who wants life and not death...Nowhere do we find the admonition to tolerate sickness and to come to terms with it."

To Remember

That God wills disease, is to me, unthinkable. That he permits it is self-evident.

—Emily Gardner Neal

To Record

To Listen

A Canaanite woman from that region came out
and cried, "Have mercy on me, O Lord, Son of
David; my daughter is severely possessed by a
demon."

—Matthew 15:22

To Ponder

Have you ever noticed that Jesus healed a lot
of the "wrong people"? A Canaanite woman, the
son of a Roman Centurion, a tax collector—
all of them social and religious outcasts! If Jesus
had appointed his disciples to act as a "screen-
ing committee," none of these people would
have made it to Jesus or the pages of the New
Testament. The disciples would have judged
them as "not worthy", just as they did the
Canaanite woman.

But Jesus never turned anyone away as "not
worthy," because moral worth was never a prerequisite for healing. He healed obvious sinners
as well as the inobvious.

To Remember

No one is ever worthy enough to be healed, nor
unworthy enough to be denied it.

To Record

March 8

To Listen

A father: "...if you can do anything, have pity on us and help us."

And Jesus said to him, "If you can!"

—Mark 9:22, 23.

To Ponder

The father of the boy who was possessed by a dumb spirit is really like many of us. He had first brought his son to Jesus' disciples while he was up on the Mount of Transfiguration. But they had been unable to heal the boy, and he had begun to believe that his son might be beyond the power of God to heal. So, he says to the Master, "If you can do anything..." and his doubts show in his words.

But Jesus knew that very often when we experience delay or what appears to be failure in healing, the problem lies, not with the giver, but the receiver.

To Remember

That something that clogs your pipeline from God is probably you.

To Record

To Listen

*"All things are possible to him who believes."
Immediately the father of the child cried out and
said, "I believe; help my unbelief."*

—Mark 9:23b, 24

To Ponder

What can be more worrisome to us in seeking
healing than the suspicion that we do not have
"enough faith"? Jesus himself linked divine
healing to "believing" or "faith."

But healing is dependent, not upon the
amount of faith we have, but upon the amount
of power we can tap with our faith. Healing can
occur even where there is a less than perfect
faith. The father of the child with the dumb
spirit had faith, but he also had nagging
doubts—just as we may. And Jesus did not require that, before he would heal his child, the
father first conquer his "unbelief."

To Remember

*A little bit of faith can release a lot of God's
healing power in my life.*

To Record

March 10

To Listen

His disciples asked him privately, "Why could we not cast it out?" And he said to them, "This kind cannot be driven out by anything but prayer."
—Mark 9:28b, 29

To Ponder

Jesus' answer to the disciples seems enigmatic. Obviously the disciples had prayed when they tried to heal the child and were unsuccessful. Furthermore, when Jesus healed the child, it appears he did so without uttering a prayer. So how can he say, "this kind cannot be driven out by anything but prayer"?

But we must remember that prayer to Jesus was not just a few well chosen words or even a well-practiced technique. For Jesus, prayer was the exercise of a close relationship with God. What the disciples—and we—need is, not a new bag of tricks or a secret knowledge, but a closer relationship with the Source of all healing power.

To Remember

Healing prayer is not a magic wand to be waved, but a vital transaction that flows from a living relationship with God.

To Record

To Listen

As rivers have their source in some far-off fountain, so the human spirit has its source. To find his fountain of spirit is to learn the secret of heaven and earth.

—Lao-tzu

To Ponder

In J. D. Salinger's *Franny and Zooey,* Zooey is discussing the "Jesus Prayer" with his sister: "but, my God, who besides Jesus really knew which end was up? *Nobody.* Not Moses. Don't tell me Moses. He was a nice man, and he kept in beautiful touch with his God and all that— but that's exactly the point. He had to keep in touch. Jesus realized there *is* no separation from God...who in the Bible knew—knew— that we're carrying the Kingdom of Heaven around with us, *inside,* where we're all too...stupid and sentimental and unimaginative to look?"

To Remember

It is the aim of the healer to stimulate the natural processes of healing that, however dormant, lie somewhere with the patient himself.

—Gordon Turner

To Record

March 12

To Listen

And all the people we saw in it are men of great stature. . . and we seemed to ourselves like grass-hoppers"

—Numbers 13:32b, 33

To Ponder

When Moses sent out some spies to recon-noiter the Promised Land, they came back with what the Bible calls "an evil report"—one in which the obstacles were said to be too great for the people of Israel. As a result of this report, they had to stay in the wilderness for 40 more years.

Jeanne Achterberg and G. Frank Lewis have conducted some significant research on the use of imagery in healing. Requiring patients to draw pictures of their disease and then their therapy, Achterberg and Lewis found that the patients whose drawings depicted the disease more powerfully than the therapy were sig-nificantly less likely to survive and experience healing.

To Remember

If we are to enter the promised land of wholeness we will need to guard against the "grasshopper complex."

To Record

To Listen

"I see men; but they look like trees, walking."
Then again he laid his hands upon his eyes; and
he looked intently and was restored."

—Mark 8:24b, 25a.

To Ponder

Although illnesses may seem to come upon us quite suddenly, the more we learn about their pathology, the more we realize that most diseases develop within us in a kind of step-by-step evolution over a considerable period of time. Usually, healing seems to follow much the same path. Thus, if it takes us a while to become ill, we ought not to be disillusioned to find that healing must follow a reversal of that same process, even though the "road back" may be at a somewhat accelerated pace.

To Remember

My healing may require "a second touch"—or more.

To Record

To Listen

For more than 6,000 times he tried again. And he succeeded in making electricity shine continuously in wire. That is faith.

> —Agnes Sanford on Edison's invention
> of the electric light.

To Ponder

Most of us would not have the perseverance that kept Edison working on the light bulb through 5,999 failures. Still, we know that few advances—scientific or spiritual—are made without some persistence. How strange, then, that some of us will try spiritual healing a few times and then give up because we don't see any results.

In Luke 5:17–26 some men wanted to bring a paralyzed friend to Jesus for healing, but the building was so jammed with people that they couldn't get in. So, "finding no way to bring him in, because of the crowd, they went up on the roof and let him down with his bed through the tiles into the midst of Jesus." Seeing their persevering faith, Jesus healed the man.

To Remember

Don't expect a thousand-dollar answer to a one-cent prayer.

To Record

To Listen

*Behold, the farmer waits for the precious fruit of
the earth, being patient over it until it receives
the early and the late rain. You also be patient.*
—James 5:7, 8

To Ponder

In healing, patience is no less golden than
perseverance. Emmett Fox tells of a little boy
who, visiting on a farm for a few days, became
fascinated with the assurance that one of the
hens would soon hatch some chicks. But after
several days of finding the eggs looking exactly
as they had the day before, the little boy began
to grow discouraged. Then, one day where
there had been eggs, he found instead some
chicks! Although the eggs had looked the same
day after day, inside there were some
wonderful changes taking place. Fox's
conclusion, "Don't hurry the chickens!", is
appropriate in healing, too.

To Remember

*Divine miracles sometimes require holy pa-
tience.*

To Record

To Listen

Now Jesus loved Martha and her sister and Lazarus. So when he heard that he was ill, he stayed two days longer in the place where he was.

—John 6:9

To Ponder

That's a fine way to show love, isn't it? If he really loved these people, wouldn't he have gone right away? Apparently Mary and Martha thought so too, for when he came to them at last, Lazarus having been dead for four days, Martha says: "Lord, if you had been here, my brother would not have died."

Jesus' reply must have been equally confusing: "Lazarus is dead, and for your sake I am glad that I was not here, so that you may believe." Perhaps they would never really understand, but, after Lazarus had been raised, they realized that, in God's own wisdom, if Jesus delayed, the blessing would be even greater.

To Remember

Healing may seem delayed when God is working at a deeper purpose or greater blessing.

To Record

To Listen

There is a lad here who has five barley loaves and two fish; but what are they among so many?
—John 6:9

To Ponder

John Ellis Large, rector of the Church of Heavenly Rest in New York, tells of rehearsing a Christmas reading he was to do on a television program. Accustomed to speaking in a huge church, he used his normal loud preaching voice and expansive gestures. During his first rehearsal, he heard the TV director's voice over the loudspeaker: "Pardon my breaking in, Dr. Large, but you don't have to reach from Manhattan to Los Angeles. Nor is it necessary for you to gesture in such an exaggerated fashion. The director is completely equipped to magnify your words and actions as needed. If you'll just quietly communicate, I'll take care of enlarging the end result."

To Remember

Our faith and love may seem all too small, but if we place what we have in his hands, he will enlarge the end result.

To Record

March 18

To Listen

All that we are is the result of what we have thought. The mind is everything. What we think, we become.

—Buddha

To Ponder

A woman was having some health problems which stemmed in part from her difficult, domineering personality. Unaware of this, the frustrated woman consulted her physician, saying: "Doctor, I must be losing my mind..." "Good!" interrupted the doctor, who had known her for many years, "The very thing you need!"

What the doctor meant, of course, was that, if she wanted to change her health, she would have to change her way of thinking. She needed to "lose" her old mind and find a new one.

In his autobiography, Yogananda records the counsel of his guru: "Really, it has been your thoughts that have made you feel alternatively weak and strong....You have seen how your health has exactly followed your subconscious expectations."

To Remember

To change my health, I may first have to change my mind.

To Record

To Listen

What a man thinketh, that is he; this is the eternal mystery

—Upanishads

To Ponder

Dr. C. Norman Shealy tells us that in his pain clinic, patients are allowed to speak about their pain only with the physician at specified appointment hours. At all other times, they are not permitted to speak of their pain. The reason is that, when we concentrate upon our pain, we intensify it. The more attention we give it, the more it seems to hurt. Dr. Shealy's patients are not asked to deny the reality of their pain, but they are asked to concentrate on something else.

So it may be with all sickness: if we concentrate upon it, we make it harder for healing to occur. The key is to fill the consciousness with something else—something that heals instead of hurts.

To Remember

If there is anything worthy of praise, think about these things.

—Philippinas 4:8b

To Record

March 20

To Listen

The arrival of one clown has a more beneficial influence on the health of a town than twenty asses laden with drugs.

—Thomas Sydenham

To Ponder

What the medical pioneer said many years ago about the healing power of humor was experienced by writer Norman Cousins when he was afflicted with a serious disease which normally proved fatal. Mr Cousins spent hours watching old motion picture comedies during his illness and found that his laughter not only raised his spirits considerably, but also registered significant results on some hospital monitoring equipment.

Some recent research indicates that when our mouths turn up in either a smile or laughter, certain beneficial chemical changes take place within our bodies.

Humor helps to make us whole.

To Remember

A cheerful heart is a good medicine, but a downcast spirit dries up the bones.

—Proverbs 17:22

To Record

To Listen

Leave your gift there before the altar and go; first be reconciled to your brother, and then come and offer your gift.

—Matthew 5:24

To Ponder

Dr. Arnold Hutschnecker tells us that "Illness is the outer expression of a deep and possibly dangerous struggle going on within." In a sense, we might say that illness is usually an indication that something is wrong in our lives. Something is out of balance. There is perhaps a disharmony with which we are not dealing.

In I Corinthians 11, Paul writes of the factions and strife in the church at Corinth. "That is why many of you are weak and ill, and some have died." The tensions and animosities in the church were reflected in health problems which some people were experiencing.

To Remember

If we seek healing, we ought first to ponder what our illness might be trying to tell us.

To Record

To Listen

You blind Pharisee! first cleanse the inside of the cup and of the plate, that the outside may also be clean.

—Matthew 23:26

To Ponder

In Jeremiah 17 there is a cryptic passage: "Heal me, O Lord, and I shall be healed . . ." At first these words seem like double-talk. But, when you ponder them, it appears that the prophet is saying that, if God heals him, then he is *really* healed. But, if someone or something else heals him, than perhaps his healing may be more an appearance than a reality. In other words, we may remove the symptoms without getting rid of the cause.

One of the "Hiroshima Maidens" who came to the USA for plastic surgery to correct her atomic bomb disfigurement said, "Tell Dr. Barsky not to worry too much if he can't give me a new face. Something has already healed inside."

To Remember

No one who has experienced a healing of the spirit would exchange what he has received for a purely physical cure.

—Emily Gardner Neal

To Record

To Listen

Whenever a person is in the wrong, he should hasten to confess his error and make amends.
—Confucius

To Ponder

Just before Christmas in 1966, producer David Merrick announced the cancellation of *Breakfast at Tiffanys*, a musical that was to have opened in 12 days with over $1 million dollars in advance ticket sales. His reason: To avoid subjecting the drama critics and theatre-going public to an excruciatingly boring evening." He went on to say, "Since the idea of adapting *Breakfast at Tiffanys* for the musical stage was mine in the first place, the closing is entirely my fault...It is my Bay of Pigs."

These last words were a reference to President John F. Kennedy's acceptance of full responsibility for the abortive Cuban invasion. For both of these men there was something "healing" in their willingness to assume responsibility for failure.

To Remember

Therefore confess your sins to one another... that you may be healed.
—James 5:16

To Record

To Listen

A person completely wrapped up in himself makes a small package. . . . The great day comes when a man begins to get himself off his hands.
—Harry Emerson Fosdick

To Ponder

Nothing is more of an obstacle to healing than to be all wrapped up in ourselves. In our understandable search for relief from the symptoms of our illness, the inconveniences and limitations it places upon us, we may become completely oblivious to others and their needs. Usually, we will be the ones most harmed by this self-centeredness. Concerned only about ourselves, we lose our perspective.

One of the happiest and most whole persons I have ever known was a woman severely afflicted with multiple sclerosis. Confined to a wheelchair, she used her telephone daily to help other people who were physically, but not spiritually, better off than she was.

To Remember

The best medicine is to stop thinking about yourself, and start thinking about other people.
—Frederic Loomis

To Record

To Listen

Come unto me all you who labor and are heavy laden, and I will give you rest.

—Matthew 11:28

To Ponder

Franklin Loehr observes that often worry creeps in in the guise of prayer. People think they are praying, but they are merely worrying in God's presence. Loehr says: "...Prayer that is 30% worry will produce 30% worry results."

The answer to the problem, however, is not to say, "Don't worry," but to heed the Psalmist's admonition to "Cast your burden upon the Lord and he will sustain you."

A reporter interviewed a woman whose husband died, leaving her with six of their children plus twelve adopted ones. To his question, "How do you manage?", she answered: "One day a long time ago I said, 'Lord, I'll do the work and you do the worrying,' and I haven't had a worry since."

To Remember

You can have worry, or you can have healing—but you can't have both.

To Record

March 26

To Listen

Jesus...marveled and said..."Truly, I say to you, not even in Israel have I found such faith."
—Matthew 10:8

To Ponder

And who is this paragon of "faith" held up to us? Answer: the most unlikely person—a Roman centurion, a man who knows nothing of Jewish religion nor Jesus, except for his reputation as a miracle worker.

But the "faith" to which Jesus refers has nothing to do with what the man believes or knows intellectually. "Faith" in this passage means *to trust.* He trusted Jesus' authority to heal.

In her long bout with tuberculosis, Catherine Marshall prayed for healing, but nothing seemed to happen. Finally, realizing that she had not surrendered herself into his hands, she told God to do with her whatever he wanted. Immediately upon surrendering herself to God, the X-rays indicated that she had begun to recover.

To Remember

Prayer is not overcoming God's reluctance, but laying hold to his highest willingness.
—Harry Emerson Fosdick

To Record

To Listen

*Then the eyes of the blind shall be opened, and
the ears of the deaf unstopped.*

—Isaiah 35:5

To Ponder

An old Arab folk tale tells us that Pestilence
once met a caravan in the desert on the road to
Baghdad. "Why must you hasten to Baghdad?"
asked the caravan chief. "To take 5,000 lives,"
was Pestilence's answer. Later, they met again
and the caravan chief said, "You deceived me,
Pestilence, instead of 5,000 lives you took
50,000." "Nay," replied Pestilence, "5,000 and
not one more—it was fear who killed the rest."

Fear can kill us in many ways. But, even if it
doesn't kill us, it greatly impedes healing.
Isaiah's messianic prophecy of miraculous
healings begins with the word "Then," for
these healings will be possible only when we
have first been healed of fear: "Strengthen the
weak hands and make firm the feeble knees."

To Remember

*Say to those who are of a fearful heart, "Be
strong, fear not!"*

—Isaiah 35:4.

To Record

To Listen

But he was in the stern asleep on the cushion; and they woke him and said to him, "Teacher, do you not care if we perish?"

—Mark 4:38

To Ponder

We have no difficulty in identifying with the panic-stricken disciples: struck by a powerful storm, their boat already taking on water and Jesus asleep in the stern!

In a moment, however, Jesus had rebuked the wind, stilled the sea, and challenged them: "Why are you afraid? Have you no faith?" Fear and unfaith are directly related. Fear is the result of not trusting God.

Dr. Joan Z. Borysenko of Boston's Beth Israel Hospital has discovered that patients who do not survive illness are those who have an "inability to relieve anxiety or depression." "Long survivors," are reported to have faith and inner confidence. Furthermore, they have a fighting spirit. They *want* to be well and *plan* to be well.

To Remember

Peace! Be still!

—Mark 8:39

To Record

To Listen

Obstacles are those frightful things we see when we take our eyes off the goal.

—Old Proverb

To Ponder

One day the wife of Robert Louis Stevenson went to his bedroom when he had been forced to put away his writing materials to stanch the life blood he was coughing away. "I suppose you will tell me that this is a glorious day," she said, knowing well his indomitable spirit. "Yes," he replied. "Strange isn't it, that I was just going to say that." Looking at the sunlight streaming through his window, he added: "I refuse to let a row of medicine bottles be the circumference of my horizon."

One thinks of Beethoven who was able to hear beyond his deafness and finish his greatest symphony, of Elizabeth Barrett Browning who was not restrained by a wheelchair. And you?—what's the circumference of your horizon?

To Remember

Our greatest joy is not in never falling, but in rising every time we fall.

—Oliver Goldsmith

To Record

March 30

To Listen

One thing I do, forgetting what lies behind and straining forward to what lies ahead, I press on toward the goal.

—Philippians 3:13, 14

To Ponder

I have dealt with more than a few people who blocked the healing they sought because they were unwilling to let go of something in their past or paralyzed by their apprehensions of the future. The philosopher Seneca wisely observed: "Some there are that torment themselves afresh with the memory of what is past; others, again, afflict themselves with the apprehension of things to come; and very ridiculously both—for the one does not now concern us, and the other not yet..." Healing is of the present moment, and if we live in the past or think only of some unknown future, we may miss the healing potential of the here and now.

To Remember

Ah, my beloved, fill the cup that clears today of past regrets and future fears.

—Omar Khayyam

To Record

To Listen

It is not well for a man to pray cream and live skim milk.

—Henry Ward Beecher

To Ponder

Do you remember the ten lepers Jesus healed? (Luke 17). Luke tells us that when Jesus told them to go and show themselves to the priests, "as they went they were cleansed."

But one of them returns to thank Jesus, who asks: "Was no one found to return and give praise to God except this foreigner?" How devoted to God we can be when we need his help! And how forgetful of him once we have received it!

Jesus says to the thankful Samaritan, "Rise and go your way; your faith has made you well." The other nine were "cleansed" of their leprosy, but the tenth was truly made whole.

To Remember

If Jesus thanked God before Lazarus was raised, shall we not thank him as we seek his healing touch?

To Record

Artist: Sharon Anderson,
Morengo, Iowa

SHARED HEALING

To be concerned only about one's own individual healing is to deny the truth that what happens to one of us happens to all of us. Indeed, each of us must share healing with those around us, with our nation, with the planet, and with the universe and beyond. Just as we find ourselves concerned with those things which make for the wholeness of body, mind, and soul, so must we extend this concern to the total domain around us because having opened ourselves to Healing Light and Love, we need to help focus that which we receive and know.

The Healing Light we're called to share and help focus is the Light of Pure Spirit and, figuratively speaking, is as bright as the light of a thousand Suns. Since the order of creation is our connectedness to the Spirit of all energy, all love and all light, we also make this connection with all forms of life, whether great or small. Somehow, when we are honest with ourselves, we know in our heart of hearts that that which we see in our sisters and brothers is also in us. Thus, by giving we are receiving and in turn will find ourselves able to give again. This creates a vibration that continues to reverberate, balancing and restoring the unity, harmony, and order that have always existed but which so often become out of tune with the music of the earthly spheres. Each day we can send out not only Healing Light and Love but also forgiveness which we in turn experience as forgiveness of self. Thus, as we act in faith, our faith is strengthened.

Our nation (be it the United States or another) calls us today to touch back into the hopes and aspirations of its early founders and leaders. In their desire for unity and harmony we find the basis for our bonding and the sure knowledge that the answers to international problems lie not in power politics or materialism but come from a deep understanding of the spiritual nature of the human being. To share our personal healing we need to extend the shaft of Healing Light and Love to the auras of those about whom we are concerned, and we need to see that light radiating over the country in which we live. Our sacred lands, waterways, atmosphere, and leaders are all in need of the healing purifying light of unconditional shared love.

This shared healing must likewise be attuned to our planet Earth, calling forth from us the same healing energy we would extend to our nation. Indeed peace and order must be returned to nature's plan of operation—a peace which comes not in opposition but rather out of the essence of Living Spirit. Then we must extend that healing love outward from our Earth, GAIA, to the universe itself, wishing it the same essential balance, the true order of life. Thus the plans that seem to evolve from millions of years of history may be likened to the ever-evolving plan of billions of galactic years in which all was and is a perfect whole to which everything ultimately comes once again.

This month, as we center our thoughts on Shared Healing, may we know more fully the Light affirmed by the words:

> " . . . the SUN of Righteousness shall rise,
> with healing in its wings."
> —Malachi 4:2b

ABOUT THE AUTHOR

L. Richard Batzler of Frederick, Maryland, has served in a government agency, as a pastor, on the faculty of a university, and as a health care professional. His contributions in community service, experiences in the healing ministry, and the authorship of his books and articles span more than thirty years. He is a Past President of SFF and is married to Evelyn Batzler.

—the Editor

To Listen

To be real, in a psychological sense, means to be integrated—integrated in thought, feeling, and bodily behavior.

—Nathaniel Branden

To Ponder

Wholeness and healing require harmony and balance between our thoughts, words, feelings and deeds. Often we become disintegrated because our deeds do not correspond to our thoughts, words or feelings. The perfection of the Christ was the absolute harmony and correspondence between these four factors. His oneness with the Father, in whom all hangs together, resulted in a oneness (wholeness) with himself.

As we strive for wellness, for integrity for ourselves and others, let us be aware of the need not only for purity and truth in each of these four factors of self, but also the need for harmonious interaction between them. And, like the Christ, let us find that harmony through our relation and response to God and His will.

To Remember

In God is life, and that life is the source of light and wholeness.

To Record

April 2

To Listen

It behooves the healers to quiet their minds enough to...become an instrument of sensing [more] than merely that which comes in through ...senses or...intellect.

—Ram Dass

To Ponder

Silence, stillness and centering are essential for entering the process and the space that brings forth the healing light. It is in the silence that we gird ourselves to meet crises and make right decisions. If we do not pause, if we continually listen to and pour out words, we will not hear that which is in the depths of our innermost being. In silence we learn to discern and to become sensitive to the kinship of all and the hurts of humanity. The concern-oriented outward life is ordered and organized from within.

To Remember

Be still and know.

To Record

To Listen

When pain is to be borne, a little courage helps more than much knowledge, a little human sympathy more than much courage, and the least tincture of the love of God more than all.

—C. S. Lewis

To Ponder

There are many ways to alleviate pain. The constant barrage of advertisers of pain medication can easily lull us into the belief that medication is the best, or even the only way. However, there are many kinds of pain, some of which no medicine can touch. Even physical pain is often the result of the deeper pain of the mind or spirit. Thus, courage, sympathy and the love of God might be just the answer for healing or reducing your pain or the pains of others. As you see others suffering, consider the underlying cause and also the cures that can come from love—your love and the love of God.

To Remember

Fear frequently fosters pain. Perfect love casts out fear.

To Record

April 4

To Listen

My friends are lazy today, considering the fact that I'm dying. They might have sent a card.
—Rudyard Kipling

To Ponder

There are so many ways that we can reach out to others in their distress. A card or call can be the difference between a good or a bad day for someone. Occasionally, such a simple remembrance may even save a life! A most important help for the hurting is a listening presence—giving the maximum of your attention with a minimum of your intention.

The technological revolution has enabled us to be in touch with others in many ways. But none of these ways can substitute for the actual human touch and physical presence. Be present as often as possible with the sick and dying—listening, touching, praying. This is the comfort that we all need and comfort which no thing can offer.

To Remember

The heart has reasons that the reason knows not of. Listen to your heart for creative ways to comfort others.

To Record

To Listen

*If ought good thou canst not say of thy brother,
foe, or friend, take thou, then, the silent way, lest
in word thou shouldst offend.*

—Anonymous

To Ponder

Words often have more power to hurt than
weapons. Yet how loosely and thoughtlessly we
use words which do hurt or even destroy lives.
Idle talk, gossip, little white lies are some of the
more common ways we use speech which
causes others distress.

One way to avoid hurting others is to take the
silent way. However, words can also heal. Better then to speak well of others, as difficult as
this may sometimes be. To see and speak of the
good in your opponents (no matter how small
the good) or those for whom you have little sympathy can raise the consciousness of healing,
affirm the positive in life and even bring about
some changes in those persons. It is another
way of loving your enemies and a way of adding healing to the universe.

To Remember

Speak the truth in love.

To Record

April 6

To Listen

Endeavor to be patient in bearing with the defects and infirmities of others, of what sort soever they be.

—Thomas A'Kempis

To Ponder

Often our impatience with others in their distresses or defects adds to their dilemmas and difficulties. Patience can be one of the greatest facilitators of healing. The patient person evidences acceptance, often silent, of the one in pain and offers assurance of on-going concern and compassion. Patience is an act of persistent, positive and purposeful power and presence. It is a promise not to forsake nor forget the ailing one.

As you face problems in dealing with others, realize that patience is a powerful fruit of the spirit that can bring peace and comfort to yourself as well as to others.

To Remember

Seeing our own shadows can help us to understand and dispel the darkness of others.

To Record

To Listen

When you stand praying, forgive...that your Father also which is in heaven may forgive you your trespasses.

—Mark 11:25, 26

To Ponder

Forgiving love lies at the heart of life. For Jesus Christ, forgiveness was the crux (cross), the crossroads, the crown of his life and teachings. His final words on the cross were those of forgiveness, and through those words and deeds healing has come to millions throughout the centuries.

Forgiveness is a resurrection experience for it breaks open the tomb of resentment, anger, and hatred which keeps us imprisoned. Forgiveness allows the healing energies of love to flow again between persons, for life to be renewed. Forgiveness can loosen the grasp of guilt which so often immobilizes.

To Remember

Forgiving is giving for another, and giving fosters living.

To Record

April 8

To Listen

Out of the millions of spheres in the universe, the one we call Earth is ours. . . . We live here. That places a responsibility on us.

—Sinio Esteve

To Ponder

We are umbilical to Earth; it is our home, our source of life. In touch and tune with nature, we experience joy, beauty, inspiration and healing. Our wellness depends greatly on how we relate to Planet Earth. If we respect and work with our planet, it will work for us. If we abuse it, we abuse ourselves. Thus, ecology is a matter of theology and of psychology. We are called to be good stewards of the earth, appreciative of the purposes and power of creation. If we can see nature as another expression of the divine, we shall find new sources of healing as we look not only upon nature, but beyond to its source.

To Remember

Earth is our mother who nurtures us. Let us love her as our own mother.

To Record

To Listen

The perfected man...does not interfere in the life of beings. He does not impose himself on them, but he "helps all beings to their freedom" (Lao-Tse).

—Martin Buber

To Ponder

Helping others is often a delicate task requiring discernment concerning the other's personhood. This involves respect for the other's freedom and wishes. Sometimes we mean to be helpful and find ourselves interfering or imposing and thereby hindering growth and healing. Thus, healing calls us to be responsible, to use all of our faculties to ascertain how we might best help without damaging the other's integrity.

Much illness is caused by limitations that persons place on themselves or limitations they allow others to place on them. If we can be catalysts, not controllers, to facilitate a person's seeing and moving beyond these limitations, we can foster healing and open up new spaces for those who are bound. To help a person, in freedom, to discover and to actualize his healing potential is one of our greatest contributions toward that person's wholeness.

To Remember

Freedom to choose is a sacred gift. Honor it.

To Record

To Listen

There are three conditions that must be present in order for a climate to be growth-promoting.... Genuineness...acceptance, or caring, or prizing...empathetic understanding.

—Carl R. Rogers

To Ponder

Genuineness in relating to others therapeutically means that one is "transparent", open, true and not beclouded with personal facade, or professionalism. There is a congruence between what is being experienced at the gut level, what is present in awareness and what is expressed to the one being helped.

Acceptance indicates a positive attitude toward the other, whatever that one is at that moment. It is an unconditional receiving of the other's distresses and dilemmas.

Empathy is "feeling into", being in touch with the other's world, expressing an understanding of what's happening in that one's life.

Healing of others thus calls for healing of self. This means being true to oneself, accepting oneself, no matter what, and being aware of and sensitive to one's own strengths and weaknesses.

To Remember

Go within. Know and respect yourself and then you can go without to meet and help others in their distress.

To Record

To Listen

Death is the supreme festival on the road to freedom.

—Dietrich Bonhoeffer

To Ponder

Death informs life. Whenever we contemplate the meaning of life, we must face the reality of death. Death is a great teacher. The universality and finality of death reveal the potentiality that death has for casting light on life's purposes. The reality of the event of death and the process of dying challenge our values, threaten our identity, modify our goals, restrict our choices, limit our control, qualify our relationships, disrupt our plans and call into question the meaning of our past, present and future. Death confronts us with our basic nature, our very selfhood, and increases our awareness, sensitivity and growth.

To Remember

Share these thoughts with others so that reflection on life's end will bring new beginnings.

To Record

April 12

To Listen

A good heart is better than all the heads in the world.

—Edward B. Lytton

To Ponder

The history of humanity reveals that much of mankind's progress has been due to the human brain and hands. These two marvelous faculties have produced ideas, languages, literature, art, music, games, tools, buildings, vehicles, weapons, and thousands of things that have improved life. But history also clearly shows the countless tragedies that have resulted from the misuse of mankind's productions. This is primarily because of the lack of heart—the absence of love and caring for others. This lack is humanity's major challenge today. The heart of the human problem is the problem of the human heart. If we do not solve it, humanity is likely to perish. Thus, all that our brains and hands produce will be of little value unless our hearts are open in love toward one another.

To Remember

If your heart is a volcano, how can blossoms bloom at your or your neighbor's feet?

To Record

To Listen

Do not be over-anxious about tomorrow, for tomorrow will bring its own cares. Enough for each day are its own troubles.

—Matthew 6:34

To Ponder

Anxiety is the source of much illness, and much anxiety comes from our living regretfully in the past and fearfully in the future. We cannot for long keep living three days at a time— yesterday, today, and tomorrow. Live today fully. Be here now. This is the message of the Christ. It is faithfulness to the present that enables us to be faithful to our future and accepting of our past. Yesterday *was* yours; it *is* God's. Tomorrow is God's secret; today is yours to live. As we realize these truths and help others to do the same, we move toward wholeness and healing for ourselves and others.

To Remember

Now is the only time you have. Live, love, laugh now.

To Record

April 14

To Listen

If a man does not keep pace with his companions, perhaps it is because he hears a different drummer.

—Henry D. Thoreau

To Ponder

Although we are all *a part of* one another, we are also *apart from* one another. Each is unique, and to recognize this uniqueness in self and others does much to promote respect, appreciation, and non-judgment toward self and others. These dynamics foster harmony, understanding, healing, compassion and open the way for creativity. They also preclude the cult of comparison which drains us of so much energy and breeds envy, jealousy and false pride. As we experience others walking different paths, let us be patient in their chosen direction and pray, whatever their paths, that the path will have a heart.

To Remember

Individuality and singularity are the serendipity of divinity. Thank God for the miracle of you and others.

To Record

To Listen

Quicken us to quicken others; ours the hand to feed our brothers; the abundance we outpour only leaves us room for more.

—Anonymous

To Ponder

To be in tune with nature is one of the greatest helps toward health and healing. One of nature's significant teachings is its lavish, continuous, and unconditional giving. And always, there is more. If you can realize this truth and express it in your everyday living, then life can be bounteous and beautiful for others and for yourself. What and how you give is your choice, but the principle is embedded in your very being—to give is to live.

To Remember

As you give to others you create a consciousness for their giving and their renewed living.

To Record

April 16

To Listen

Get thee out of thy country. . .unto a land that I will show thee.

—Genesis 12:1

To Ponder

All that is worthwhile in life involves risk. The Bible is the recital of the mighty acts of God and of persons' risking in response to God's challenges. We grow and help others grow toward wholeness as we, in faith, offer and risk ourselves as living sacrifices for the good. Illness often comes because of our fears, our hesitations to share, care, and dare. The ultimate risk is to share with others the heavenly bread of our self-being—which is the supreme act of communion. As we responsibly share our lives with others, we and they discover that far country, that Promised Land.

To Remember

We start near to go far. Center on God and then go forth to strike a trail for others.

To Record

To Listen

I live not in myself, but I become portion of that around me.

—Lord Byron

To Ponder

Throughout the centuries, persons in various walks of life have affirmed the truth of the kinship of all life. In our time when the communication and transportation revolutions, and the many other technologies have brought life in all of its forms closer together and revealed the interrelationships, we need to be aware of our thinking, speaking and acting. For each of these activities can affect others positively or negatively. In terms of human life, before speaking or acting, a good rule is to THINK in this way: Is what I say or do True, Helpful, Important, Necessary, Kind? Such THINKing will do much for others and self.

To Remember

I am a part of all that is. What I think, say, and do is cosmically important.

To Record

April 18

To Listen

I have opened my doors to the wayfarer.

—Job 31:32

To Ponder

Ours is a day of the wayfarer. This is the age of the refugee, the dispossessed, the homeless. This phenomenon is one of humanity's greatest ills and shames. It speaks of human greed, will to power, insensitivity, cruelty—all of which are sicknesses of the soul. We can facilitate healing for others as we open the "doors" of our hands, hearts and wallets to those who cry out for a door to shelter, food and work. The doors we open to others open new doors of healing and wholeness for ourselves.

To Remember

What door can I open today for someone who is "shut out" somewhere?

To Record

To Listen

To act effectively is to realize that there is a guide for action that far outshines the tiny thought, "I must do something."... If you do not know what to do, then you might want to try doing nothing.
—Alan Cohen

To Ponder

Life is rhythmic—inflow and outflow, day and night, systolic and diastolic. This is the pattern of the universe, and as part of the universe, we need to recognize, accept and act within this pattern. We stress ourselves and others when we constantly believe or feel that we need to give, go, etc. There is a natural need to be still, to do nothing and to listen to all those sounds we can't hear.

Silence and stillness can be the center and womb of creativity, clarity, and commitment. It is this creative *nothingness* that often sounds the clearest note of *somethingness* and provides for us the way, truth, and life.

To Remember

In the silence, let go and let God.

To Record

April 20

To Listen

I have not arrived at my understanding of the universe through the thinking mind.
                              —Albert Einstein

To Ponder

Thinking and feeling, though inseparably related, are two distinct faculties of persons. Throughout the ages discussions have been carried out concerning which is the more important. Which of these one considers the more important often depends on one's values, priorities and life orientation. Generally, females have been considered more intuitive and emotional; males more intellectual and rational. Recent brain-mind research and various psychological theories tend to acknowledge these emphases. If true, this could mean that more balance, harmony and healing can come if females seek to develop their male aspects, and males do the same for their female aspects. If this is done on the inner plane of one's selfhood, then those outer disharmonies and conflicts which exist not only between males and females, but also within entire societies and cultures, might well diminish.

To Remember

The way is found when our maleness and femaleness walk together in peace.

To Record

To Listen

The individual realizes that he is part of an infinite scheme, his own life playing its measured part in the divine plan.

—Silver Birch

To Ponder

When we consider the universe in all of its magnitude and multitude, it is easy to feel a sense of personal insignificance and even meaninglessness. The order, processes, constancy and marvels of creation reveal plan and purpose, even in spite of our own thoughts and feelings about our part in creation. The prevention of personal distresses, whether of body, mind or spirit, as well as the healing of these aspects, can come by our trusting and living with the belief that we—as a part of the universe—have purpose. Even though we may not fully understand our purpose, to believe that we do have a purpose can motivate us to live joyfully and harmoniously with all of life and to better accept that which happens to us. This is not a fatalistic nor deterministic attitude, but one that enables us to better meet life no matter what. It can also move us to understand, appreciate and help others in their trials and their triumphs.

To Remember

You are an expression, a manifestation of the Creator and as such you are worthwhile.

To Record

April 22

To Listen

If you are serious about the sufferings of man-kind, you must perfect the only source of help you have—yourself.

—Jerome Frank

To Ponder

One of the most poignant passages in the New Testament is the word of Jesus who said, "Be perfect as your Father in heaven is perfect." This is one of those perennial philosophy priorities which has been expressed in many ways. Peace, joy, love, forgiveness and all of the other blessings that we might wish to share with others have their origin within our self. This does not mean that we wait until we think we are perfect before reaching out to others, but that we keep on the path toward personal perfection as we seek to help them.

Christ's comment puts the focus on the locus of that perfection—God. As we seek to know, love and serve God, we move toward perfection, and, as that happens, we automatically are directed to our brothers and sisters. As we seek first the Kingdom of God (perfection), we will be given gifts for healing others.

To Remember

Love mercy, do justly, and walk humbly with your God.

To Record

To Listen

The glory of friendship . . . is the spiritual inspiration that comes to one when . . . someone else believes in him and is willing to trust him with his friendship.

—Ralph Waldo Emerson

To Ponder

To accept the fact that we are accepted is a basic ingredient of faith and trust. So often when we have not been true to ourselves and, in a sense, have become alienated from ourselves, we find it difficult to believe that anyone can accept us. When we see this condition in another, we can be an instrument of healing if we affirm our acceptance of that person, even though we may not approve of that one's behavior. This may involve turning the other cheek or going that extra mile, but in so doing we set up the condition for renewal and hope. This takes courage and involves risk, but so it is with all that is worthwhile in life.

To Remember

To miss a need may be to miss a miracle. Live in your house by the side of the road and be a friend to man.

To Record

April 24

To Listen

The world is too much with us;...getting and spending we lay waste our powers; little we see in nature...; we have given our hearts away.

— William Wordsworth

To Ponder

While many are rightly concerned about the question of overkill (arms race), there is emerging another dangerous, yet more subtle phenomenon—overskill. Our technology has created new problems in unemployment, depersonalization, ethics, education and human behavior. Things (the world) are becoming our kings; machines, our masters.

The wonders and blessings of nature offer a beautiful balance to our metal, concrete and plastic world. Earth, sky, and sea, moment by moment, offer their renewing and healing energies for our bodies, minds, and spirits.

Walk often with friend, relative, the poet, or just alone into the world of nature and find that world in a grain of sand or a wild flower which can take you beyond this world to new dimensions of reality that expand and ennoble your life.

To Remember

Hug a tree; thank a green plant; smile with the sunrise; soar with the stars.

To Record

To Listen

Some men die by shrapnel, some go down in flames, but most perish inch by inch in play at little games.

—Author unknown

To Ponder

In a world beset with gimmicks, gadgets, grab-bags and games, most of which we really don't need, we become more and more tranquilized by trivia.

Countless producers of paraphernalia, and purveyors of products paw over us, prey on us and persistently try to persuade us that life can best be beautiful by using their product. In this barrage of bargains, boasting and braggadocio, we get caught up in illusions (separation from truth through our senses), delusions (separation from truth through our minds), collusion (separation from truth by combining illusion and delusion)—all of which lead to confusion, the separation of self from Self. This trivilization of reality results in emptiness, frustration, boredom, depression, and often, suicide.

Perhaps more than ever before, we need to be discerning and decisive in our perceptions and conceptions to keep our balance and also to help others keep theirs.

To Remember

To know who and why you are is a key to wholeness and a priority for living.

To Record

April 26

To Listen

We all have reservoirs of life to draw upon, of which we do not dream.

—William James

To Ponder

A major source of distress among persons is the lack of self-esteem and self-worth. To a great extent, this is due to an unawareness of the virtually unlimited potentialities they possess. For centuries those who work in the spiritual and mental sciences have affirmed and elucidated this truth. Yet many do not know or do not heed this wisdom which often is the difference between sickness and health. For those who know and live by this truth, one of the best ways to help is to awaken others to their potential and encourage them to actualize that potential. A key to self-actualization is not to set limits on self, or allow others to set limits on you.

To Remember

As you help others discover and manifest their potentials, you will discover and actualize your own.

To Record

To Listen

*Hugging is ecologically sound, energy-efficient,...
is portable, keeps on giving benefits after-the-
fact....*

—Source unknown

To Ponder

Touching is one of our greatest healing gifts.
Through touching (hugging, stroking, massag-
ing, nuzzling, gentling, etc.) lives have been
saved, growth facilitated, diseases healed, sor-
rows comforted and hopes renewed. Today we
are closer together through our technology,
yet we touch each other less and less. Like ships
in the night, we so often pass without even a
glance, much less a word or a touch. Our fast
pace of life blurs the images of pain and pathos
in countenances so that we not only do not see
faces, but even more, fail to understand hearts.
Fears and lack of love often result in "bad"
touches as children, spouses and the elderly
more and more become abused.

Anguishing and lonely humanity needs more
hugs, more tender touches.

To Remember

*Do not hug someone tomorrow whom you could
hug today. Remember that when you give a hug
(or touch), you get one in return.*

To Record

April 28

To Listen

See yourself in others. Then whom can you hurt? What harm can you do?

—The Buddha

To Ponder

Understanding others is a way of promoting health and healing. A step in that understanding is doing unto others as you would have them do unto you. Or, in psychological terms, doing a role reversal—putting yourself in the other's place. Many times in our relationships we seek to elevate ourselves by lowering or diminishing others. This envy or enmity becomes our enemy.

Everyone has goodness by virtue of having been created in God's image. If we can discover and affirm this goodness in others, no matter how slight, we simultaneously activate our own goodness and promote peace. It is our focusing on the negativities of others that brings fear and conflict. At the center of our being we discover that all are one. Go deep within, and discover this oneness. Then you will see others in a new light which can dispel the darkness of discord, distress, and despair.

To Remember

Not in the looking glass, but in the face of others I see my real self.

To Record

To Listen

Loneliness, far from being a rare and curious phenomenon, is the central and inevitable fact of human existence.

—Thomas Wolfe

To Ponder

Loneliness has many faces. It appears in alienation, in the isolation of the disabled, during illness and after the death of a loved one, in loss of faith, in misunderstanding, in pioneering and frontier-type endeavors, in waiting, in poor self-image and in many other experiences. Loneliness is not always aloneness. There is much in the solitary that is creative and beneficial.

Since loneliness is universal and often destructive, it behooves us to be aware of the dynamics and dimensions of the loneliness of others and ourselves. Through this awareness we can often help others to find new purpose, joy and healing for body, mind and spirit.

To Remember

To realize the all-oneness of life will help to heal the pains of a-loneness.

To Record

To Listen

The risk of extinction,. . . embracing as it does the life and death of every human being on earth and every future human being, transcends all other issues.

—Jonathan Schell

To Ponder

Built into human civilizations is a hierarchy of priorities. We frequently find ourselves out-of-sorts because we ignore or distort priorities in living. This involves clarification of values and setting of goals—two "musts" in the process of attaining and maintaining whole-ness.

The signs of our times are revealing the necessity to prioritize. We not only dissipate our energies and talents when we fail to clarify and to decide on values and goals, but also, we move closer to total dis-ease, the destruction of humanity itself. It may at times be important what you acquire for your daily well-being, but not to the exclusion of consideration of those ultimate realities that affect our very existence. Pay your light bill, but also pay attention to the growing darkness cast by those sources and forces which threaten our lives.

To Remember

Let not the H-bomb be the final sequel in which all are cremated equal.

To Record

SURVIVAL OF CONSCIOUSNESS

Since the beginning of time, one of the great questions for humanity has been, if a person dies shall he or she live again. All people, at one time or another, ponder this question. It is also a basic question which religion has always sought to answer. The word survival comes from the root *vivere* which means "to live"—that is, to continue to live or exist. Consciousness comes from *con* and *sciere* which literally mean "to know" and have to do with the awareness, perception or knowledge of a psychological or spiritual fact lying deep within the self.

This metaphysical question of survival has also been the basis for the beginnings of Psychical Research—do we survive death; will we live again, and will the soul aspect of our physical being continue in another state of consciousness? Such a state could be described in various ways: as the Communion of Saints, as the concept of Life after Life with the spirit reincarnating, or even as a merging with the vast whole. Any of these can be a possible reality for the many peoples scattered around the Universe.

Life beyond the grave must also mean life before birth, for to be immortal means to be from everlasting to everlasting. The "I" that we are is separate and apart from personality or the physical body. It is the spiritual "I" which gives us the secret of the eternality and immortality of life. Interestingly, observations of death-bed experiences have shown us that the consciousness which survives grows stronger as the body grows weaker. Often doctors, nurses and attendants are aware that patients are strongest just before death.

Actually, for centuries people have had experiences which have led them to conclude that there is consciousness outside the physical body. Primitive tribesmen out on a hunt knew how to send messages back telling those at home to make preparation for the cleaning process. Likewise the villagers know when the hunt was unsuccessful. We today are recognizing that through "remote viewing" we too can observe what is happening in far away places by sending our minds out to those locations.

Other experiences have helped convince us of the existence of consciousness and the power of the mind. These include: out-of-body experiences, mediumship, past-life memories, and near-death experiences. Studies in the areas of cultural anthropology, comparative religion and parapsychology also seem to indicate the universality of the evidence in favor of the survival of consciousness.

Although in the past science observed the universe in terms of matter/energy (the brain) giving rise to mind, today many scientists recognize a dualistic view, accepting not only a concept of matter/energy (mind) but also a concept of matter (mind) spirit. Science explores with its matter/energy, but mind/spirit is more subjective and brings the inner world into the exploratory process.

Eventually, we may all come to an understanding similar to that of the metaphysician of old who felt that consciousness was here first, and from consciousness (mind) has evolved matter. Thus, survival will be a matter of remembering, and someday we may remember the answer to Job's question—"If a man die, shall he live again?" (Job 14:14). Perhaps then we'll be able to say:

> I shall not die, but live and declare
> the works of the Lord.
>
> Psalm 118:17

ABOUT THE AUTHOR

Paul Lambourne Higgins was the first president and co-founder of Spiritual Frontiers Fellowship. He enjoyed a distinguished career as a Methodist clergyman and orator, and he has utilized his experience as a world traveler to write a series of books for Prentice-Hall. Called "Pilgrimages" the books are fascinating guides to the Holy Places throughout the world. Co-director, with his wife Ruth, of the Rockport Colony, Paul lives in Rockport, Massachusetts overlooking the water.

—the Editor

To Listen

For now we see through a glass darkly; but then face to face.

—I Corinthians 13:12

To Ponder

When St. Paul writes of the physical body, and the spiritual body, he identifies the latter with the permanent self, with its memories, aspirations, and love. While here on earth we see ahead dimly (in certain enlightened moments), but then (after the transition) it shall be face to face. The spiritual body, freed from the pressures of the physical, finds dormant faculties awakening with the coming into a larger level of being. Rudolf Steiner speaks of three bodies, physical, etheric, astral, and how at physical death the etheric (organizing self) and astral (spiritual self) unite, moving on in the continuing journey of the soul. Jesus himself made many references to the transition from this level to the next and asked for our trust.

To Remember

Ye believe in God, believe also in me.

To Record

May 2

To Listen

Life is real, life is earnest,
And the grave is not the goal.
Dust thou art, to dust returneth,
Was not spoken of the soul.
                    —Henry Wadsworth Longfellow

To Ponder

This great American poet is giving a meaningful answer to the ages-old question posed by Job: "If a man die, shall he live again?" Longfellow clarifies our thinking: the word, Die, if applied to a human being, cannot mean, extinction. The body may *die*, and return to dust—but not the soul, for it's eternal. We must recognize that death, as applied to our personhood, our self, is a fallacy, an error.

Many are now saying, "so-called death," realizing that for the soul, its body's demise merely frees one for an altered state of consciousness in which the handicaps and pains of the physical no longer exist.

Yes, Job, if a man die, he *continues* to live, without his spirit ever missing a moment of life.

To Remember

Who are we? We are spirits.

To Record

To Listen

We do not "give up the ghost"! Rather, we, the spirits, "shuffle off this mortal coil"—the ghost gives up the body!

—Frank C. Tribbe

To Ponder

Sayings from our culture often become part of our philosophy of life without our having consciously chosen it to be so. When you find yourself parroting from folklore, stop to question whether you really believe what you are saying. Some phrases and affirmations that we unconsciously adopt in this way are sound and helpful—some, not.

But repetition of sayings—good or bad—is a form of affirmation, and affirmations drill automatic attitudes into one's deepest Being. Do we really want to give up the spirit at death, or is it the body we'd like to let go? Shakespeare's Hamlet considered very carefully "what dreams may come when we have shuffled off this mortal coil." He understood the powerful reality of the afterlife.

To Remember

We are spirits! At death, we will give up our bodies.

To Record

May 4

To Listen

What is it that survives? Personal identity... in an embodied existence, with his own memories... and full accessibility of subliminal memories.
—Hornell Hart

To Ponder

Spiritual "embodiment" was a real problem for the early Christian church, nor had the Jews of Jesus' day understood it. Fortunately, for us, the apostle Paul somehow received true enlightenment in the desert, and his writings speak clearly to modern man. He wrote of the "spirit body" housing the soul after physical death. Now, psychical research confirms a nonmaterial part of the Self which goes out-of-body while the physical body lives and, after death, materializes at times, appears apparitionally, and does physical things like stopping clocks.

More importantly, Professor Hart saw that the surviving entity had the same personality, the same conscious memories and, most special of all, had those subliminal memories that, during physical life, had been lost to consciousness.

To Remember

Personality, embodiment, conscious memory, subliminal memory. What more could we want?

To Record

To Listen

Because of the testimony of science to a rational and trustworthy universe, I believe that I shall survive physical death.

—Sherwood Eddy

To Ponder

Of course, nowhere near a majority of scientists is presently willing to interpret that testimony as strong evidence for survival of physical death. But the testimony is there. And Sherwood Eddy found it to be evidence capable of supporting his belief. There must always be an element of faith, but that testimony of science can undergird our knowledge and beliefs, so that only a small leap of faith is required.

That testimony of science comes from more than a hundred years' of psychical research and parapsychology by some of our most competent scientists, using *strict* scientific method. Eddy was especially impressed that that testimony demonstrated a "rational and trustworthy universe" that did not operate by chance.

To Remember

It's comforting to have a rational and trustworthy universe—with God in control.

To Record

May 6

To Listen

Evidence of a world beyond is vast, various, and at times confusing. . . . But, let us live and die as if we were immortal.

—Martin Ebon

To Ponder

The inference to be drawn from Mr. Ebon's words is an urging, to the more timid among us, to put our faith to work—to live and ultimately to die upon the working hypothesis that we are indeed immortal beings. That will make for a glorious life and a death with exciting expectations.

So what, that we can't prove it! Precious few certainties of any sort do we have. But we do have evidence—lots of it—strong evidence—of a world beyond. So, let us accept that evidence, in spite of its uncertainties, and step out in faith. We'll not live to regret our belief in immortality! And if it's true, we'll be a whole world ahead!

To Remember

Step out in faith! Believe in immortality.

To Record

To Listen

Science without religion is lame; religion without science is blind.

—Albert Einstein

To Ponder

The science of parapsychology has *not proved* the fact of spirit survival of bodily death. It is unlikely that science ever will *prove* survival. However, parapsychology and other fringes of orthodox science have given us much data in recent years from which thoughtful persons can legitimately glean *evidence for survival.* That is for many of us a substantial pedestal of knowledge, from which only a small "leap of faith" is required. What a difference from the position of our grandparents a half-century ago, whose belief in survival had to be totally a matter of faith.

And when we ponder upon that situation, might we not say, "that's good"?—for perhaps faith rather than certainty is the way it should be in crucial matters of religion.

To Remember

Science is undergirding our faith, not taking its place, and that's good.

To Record

May 8

To Listen

Go to my brethren and say to them, I am ascending to my Father and your Father, to my God and your God.

—John 20:17

To Ponder

The significance of the spiritual self (with its extrasensory perception and awakened capacities) can be seen in the Biblical accounts of the Transfiguration of Christ, and, supremely so, of course, in the Resurrection, which is the heart of Christianity. These great narratives of the New Testament are at the basis of our Christian Apostolic doctrine of the Communion of Saints, to which we give affirmation in the historic creeds, and wherein we recognize and communicate with those who have passed through physical death. Even great souls from the Higher Heavens, like Moses and Elijah, appeared in that wondrous seance atop Holy Mount Tabor and were witnessed by Peter and John and James. Indeed these experiences are the birthright of the soul, an aspect of its universal light.

To Remember

Blessed are those who have not seen and yet believe.

To Record

To Listen

The spiritual component in man that has been demonstrated in the laboratories...is certainly non-material. It cannot "die."

—Alson J. Smith

To Ponder

When young Jim Pike came to his father, the Episcopal bishop, he voiced the same regret as every suicide communicating from beyond the Veil: nothing is solved by suicide—the problems must *still* be dealt with. The International Association for Near Death Studies has the same report from unsuccessful suicides who went into the next world, but were brought back by modern resusitation. All said the Spirit of man cannot die, and we will have less pain if we deal with our problems in this physical life.

Many of us have never considered or tried suicide. But we may procrastinate in handling our problems. Since we are non-material spirits, let us solve our problems and put our houses in order before moving into the spiritual realms.

To Remember

I am spirit—I cannot die!

To Record

May 10

To Listen

The hypothesis of survival is not only justified as a working theory, but is actually the only one capable of rationally explaining the facts.

—Herward Carrington

To Ponder

The author, a psychical researcher, concludes that the phenomena of extrasensory perception, especially telepathy and clairvoyance, are not an alternative to survival, but a virtual guarantee of it. He further points out that no amount of extrasensory perception on the part of a psychic-sensitive can affect or explain away the strong and certain evidence for survival that is provided by phenomena such as "direct voice" communications or materializations recorded on tape and by photography in the seance room.

Although spirit communications, especially those received through mediums, are suspect in the view of skeptics because of the possibility of fraud or subliminal ESP, it is inconceivable that the cross-correspondences recorded in England by a dozen sensitives could be so explained.

To Remember

Do we think? Then, survival is the answer.

To Record

To Listen

Some reports describe only what can be observed from the threshold; they are glimpses into a next world, not journeys into the interior.

—Paul Beard

To Ponder

Not all kinds of evidence that bear upon the problems of the future life are equal. Out-of-body experiences tell us little more than the probability we have a non-physical component that might survive death of the body, since it can survive separation from the body (but, of course, this is important, too).

Deathbed visions; crisis visions and communications (immediately after a distant death); precognitive death visions; and the near-death or clinical death experiences—all form the group which Beard classes as observations from the threshold of death—they are valid and important, but they are not journeys into the interior. They are the new arrival's impressions from the threshold, not the appraisal of a long-time resident.

To Remember

Understand the kinds of survival evidence—but believe in the result.

To Record

May 12

To Listen

Deathbed visions do happen. They are not "hal-
lucinations"; they are not caused by drugs, not
the result of senility.

—Karlis Osis

To Ponder

Next time you learn of friend or relative
seemingly on their deathbed, when visiting, pay
attention to glimpses they report of the next
life—ask if they are having such, even if they
don't volunteer it. Almost always they will be
eager to tell this experience to a simpatico lis-
tener. If such a report is forthcoming, ask questions about the experience—*how* did they know
they were seeing a certain one?—and was there
any communication?

These visions may come with eyes open or
closed; the visitation may come during sleep,
disguised as an ordinary dream. And, more and
more, we are beginning to believe that in the
last hours of earthly life the dying person may
be slipping back and forth across "the line."

To Remember

Ask dying loved ones about spirit visitors and
their own visits across the line.

To Record

To Listen

Death is painless and pleasant!...No matter how disagreeable the preliminaries...actual death is easy, and usually welcome.

—Archie Matson

To Ponder

If your dying loved ones believe in spirit survival of bodily death, their only big concerns are usually your grief and loss and their own pain. You can help them much by avoiding discussion or the obvious appearance of your own grief. Of course, assure them they will be truly missed, but don't dwell on this issue—don't make them feel guilty for your grief.

If you succeed in handling these points well, then try to assure them that death itself is pain-free. Dying may be very painful in some situations, but it may help your loved one if you emphasize that death itself is not only painless, but actually pleasant! Release of a pain-racked body will be a special relief in death.

To Remember

There is no pain in death—do not fear it.

To Record

To Listen

Don't say, "He died"—rather, "He was reborn"—born out of his body and out of space-time into full spiritual fellowship with God.

—Roy A. Burkhart

To Ponder

And don't say he is *gone* or *passed away.* In the realm of Spirit there is no place, and your loved one still lives and is still here. This author suggests that man will experience three births— one into the physical body, a second into spiritual awareness (conversion), and a third out of the physical body into the "fourth dimension."

The deceased loved one is now limited only by the degree of his illumination—and that will increase as his spirit progresses. Remember, you never saw *him* before death; you saw his body, but you *experienced* him. You still can. No one ever saw God, but many have experienced him.

To Remember

The greatest birth of them all: death!

To Record

To Listen

Evidence... indicates that over-mourning, over-grief, and exaggerated sadness can hold the so-called "dead" back from entering into a happiness which they would otherwise have.

—Leslie D. Weatherhead

To Ponder

Dr. Weatherhead (British Methodist clergyman) wrote from a lifetime of ministry, deep study, and a complete awareness of the findings of psychical research. His concern is very valid, for research data indicate strongly that the largest factor in creation of earthbound/disturbed excarnates is unthinking conduct by families left behind, which ties them to the earth-plane and distresses them with concerns that belong to the "living," not the "dead."

There's nothing wrong or sinful about grief. It's very real, natural, and serves as catharsis. Also, grief is a very personal thing and there is no standard time-frame in which it should run its course. But if the mourner is mindful of the handicap thus imposed on the "departed," he may work through it sooner.

To Remember

An early end to grief speeds departed loved ones on their way.

To Record

To Listen

Only the body dies. The self or spirit, or whatever you may wish to label it, is eternal.

—Elizabeth Kubler-Ross

To Ponder

More and more, we find science and religion singing in harmony. Dr. Ross is speaking as a scientist—a research psychiatrist. Medical doctors and other scientists now know there is something more to a human than the physical body, even though many of them still are uncomfortable in calling that something more, a soul. Something lives on. Something can sometimes communicate to us from the Great Beyond.

Are you receptive to communication from departed ones? Do you pray for their spiritual progression? When you think of them, is it in a positive vein, so that your thoughts will support their progress rather than hold them back? If there is the slightest reason for doing so, ask their forgiveness for your inadequacies when they were here.

To Remember

We are eternal spirits.

To Record

To Listen

Death is no tragedy! We are immortal spirits, temporarily living in physical bodies. Our life-styles should be consciously framed accordingly.
—Frank C. Tribbe

To Ponder

One of our built-in attitudes in this civilization is the *assumption* that death is a tragedy. But death is but a doorway to an altered state of consciousness, and we are just in the first stage of eternal life. Don't carry the handicap of a short-sighted lifestyle through that doorway. Death should be a promotion for the dying.

Throughout the New Testament, references by Jesus and his disciples to "death" are metaphorical—spiritually, death means separation from God. And separation is by our initiation—God doesn't leave us, and he's always available when we are ready to *live* again in harmony with him.

To Remember

Live in the here and now, so that your "death" can merit a celebration.

To Record

May 18

To Listen

We were in being long before the foundations of the world; we existed in the eye of God.

—St. Clement of Alexandria

To Ponder

For some persons preexistence means reincarnation. Preexistence, however, is not necessarily limited to this view, or to this world. Essentially it is the recognition of our coming from God, that we are spiritual beings with earlier origins. We remember Wordsworth's lines from his *Intimations of Immortality*:

> Our birth is but a sleep and a forgetting;
> The Soul that rises with us, our life's Star,
>   Hath had elsewhere its setting,
>   And cometh from afar.
>   Not in entire forgetfulness,
>   And not in utter nakedness,
> But trailing clouds of glory do we come
> From God, who is our home.

To Remember

Preexistence *and* survival are one continuum.

To Record

To Listen

The true nature of God cannot...be grasped by the finite mind....Can it be possible that we...are linked with all this?

—Harold Sherman

To Ponder

Linkage—that is the key. It probably was implied by Jesus, saying the Kingdom of Heaven is within—he and the Father were one—he is in us and we in him. Interconnectedness is the great Truth. We are linked to each other, to all life and God. So, we are immortal and can never die. Our apparent separateness from each other and from God is illusion, born of our physicality.

George Russell, Irish mystic-poet, using the pseudonym, AE, wrote: "There are corridors in the House of our Being, leading into the hearts of others, and windows which open into eternity, and we hardly can tell where our own Being ends and another begins, or if there is any end to our Being."

To Remember

Interconnectedness with God and with all life? Live like it!

To Record

May 20

To Listen

If inquiry into life after death were only to consist of an anticipatory look forward, it could be little more than curiosity.

—Paul Beard

To Ponder

His previous book, *Survival of Death*, established the probability of survival; Beard now considers what the hereafter is like. This sort of survival research is important, since the searcher will one day embark on his own journey into the afterlife; so, as any prudent explorer, he can now learn about the far country, and may recognize that his daily creation of a life pattern is creating his explorer's equipment for that future journey.

This attitude should make one take a longer view—and might alter one's time-scale and one's scale of values. Rather than a gulf between this world and the next, Beard suggests there's an inner world to which men belong both before and after death, in which the same spiritual laws apply.

To Remember

Knowledge about the hereafter helps to prepare for living there.

To Record

To Listen

When John Keats, at twenty-six, was about to move to the other side, he said, "And now I'll be with the English poets."

—John Keats

To Ponder

The lines of communication are open between this world and the next, and at divinely appointed times the glorious breakthrough comes. William Blake tells of how he talked with those Beyond; the great saints tell the same, and some of us can relate our experiences also. What glorious links we have with the eternal world. The Other Worlds impinge upon this one, and we suddenly know that we are all one in a Divine order, and we rejoice in the everlastingness of life. When such experiences are ours, we want to share the Good News with others. This is what the Gospel means. "Heaven connected with earth! The union of mortal with immortal," as John Wesley says.

To Remember

The Eternal reigns, and in that divine love we find ourselves.

To Record

May 22

To Listen

*The future condition on the other side. . .will. . .
be. . .the expression under new conditions of the
prevailing bent of our present life.*
                    —Archdeacon Basil Wilberforce

To Ponder

The Bible, especially when seen in the light of
the mystical, has much to reveal about life after
death. The spirit of man is "at school in the
body" while on earth. In this continuity of life
we make our choices, influencing in large
measure our own destiny. Having made the
transition, we carry with us the continuing
quality of our life on earth into the next stage,
even as Jesus indicates in His parable of Dives
and Lazarus (Luke 16:19–31). The Pauline doctrine holds true, that *whatsoever a man soweth,
that shall he also reap* (Galatians 6:7). Yet this
concept is only part of the picture; it is tem-
pered in the knowledge that Divine Love can
break through and change our whole course.

To Remember

*There is One who breaks the power of sin and
sets us free.*

To Record

To Listen

And Jesus said unto him, Verily I say unto thee,
Today shalt thou be with me in paradise.

—Luke 24:23

To Ponder

Where are we after the death of the physical
body? We go at once to the next level of life for
which we are prepared.

The Church Fathers and John Wesley reaf-
firm this biblical principle, and so does modern
psychical research. In Christ we find a joyous
state called paradise as soon as we leave the old
physical body. Indeed there are levels beyond
this.

Sometimes we have a foretaste of paradise.
When my beloved father-in-law was approach-
ing death, he told me of the beautiful experience he was having on the Other Side. "It is
all as we have talked about, only more wonderful. Pray that I leave this physical body soon, so
I can freely enjoy this greater life. I am already
there in spirit."

To Remember

The good life is ours now to enjoy, and the in-
finitely greater life awaits us.

To Record

To Listen
Survival may prove to be a long-term opportunity to qualify for immortality.

—Paul Beard

To Ponder

This philosophy would separate questions of bare spirit survival from the issue of immortality. It is a somewhat disquieting thought—especially for those who smugly quote the theology of "once saved, always saved," and lead a selfish (and possibly, sinful) earthlife. It meets the objection of scholars who, looking at man's "stumbling imperfect self," ask if most personalities aren't too worthless to survive death?

Thus, Beard suggests (based on research evidence) that all survive, but that "surely a man must do much more than merely die" in order to qualify for immortality. He looks upon immortality as a process of *becoming*, and says that qualifying for immortality may be a very long-term process indeed, and the qualifying process may very well begin on earth.

To Remember
The sooner we start preparing to qualify for immortality, the better.

To Record

To Listen

In my Father's house are many mansions; if it were not so, I would have told you.

—John 14:3

To Ponder

While there are various interpretations of this famous passage from St. John's Gospel, a very old and revered one is that the reference "many mansions" is to the many abodes in the world beyond on the soul's pilgrimage toward an increasing knowledge and love of God. Each abode on the pilgrim's journey is a haven, where there is rest and work and joy, a mingling with old friends and meeting new ones, with plans for greater things ahead. It is a level of consciousness. From one abode the pilgrim moves to another, always with the assurance that Christ has prepared a place for him and has opened the Way. In every abode, at every level, God is near.

To Remember

I go to prepare a place for you.

To Record

To Listen

Where I am going you cannot follow me now; but you shall follow afterward.

—John 14:36

To Ponder

This firm promise by Jesus leaves no doubt of the certainty of the afterlife; a few hours later he made a similar statement to the thief, saying, "Today you will be with me in paradise." He did not provide detailed descriptions of the hereafter, but Jesus left no doubt of its reality. The parable of the rich man and the beggar mentioned the afterlife; the Transfiguration event gives powerful evidence for its reality.

Throughout his ministry, Jesus referred to his return to the Father, and steps he would be taking there. The apostles couldn't believe that departure would come soon, yet he repeatedly told them so. After the ascension by Jesus, his followers preached the heavenly kingdom and many went willingly to martyrs' deaths.

To Remember

Our place in the hereafter is assured.

To Record

To Listen

O Sabbath rest by Galilee! O calm of hills above!
Where Jesus knelt to share with thee the silence
of eternity, interpreted by love.
　　　　　　　　　　　—John Greenleaf Whittier

To Ponder

There is a holy mountain in the Holy Lands, Mount Tabor, where Jesus took Peter and James and John. There Jesus was transfigured, and the disciples saw Moses and Elijah of old appear, and heard the Divine voice from on High. It was a celestial experience, this amazing seance, when those souls who had departed this earth centuries earlier returned to be with Jesus and his three disciples. Some of us have had this kind of a wonderful breakthrough from the Eternal world, showing the closeness between the spiritual world and this world.

We attest to this experience in the words of the Apostles' Creed.

To Remember

I believe in the communion of saints.

To Record

May 28

To Listen

You awake; you arise; you have no more to do with these past transient shadows;... See, all is real here! All is permanent; all eternal.

—John Wesley

To Ponder

Paradise is that level of life after death into which we can awake. Life there and here are really closely related; it is the awakening of the individual consciousness that opens up to the beauty and joy and love in both. Indeed the two worlds often seem to interpenetrate.

Once when I was conducting Holy Communion and was cast down because so few people had come to receive the Bread of Life, I was suddenly lifted up and inspired when we came to the Preface to the Sanctus. Out of the corner of my eye as I faced the Altar, I saw a Spanish priest of another age, clad in his beautiful vestments giving me his blessing. He was a messenger from Paradise.

To Remember

Awake, thou that sleepest!

To Record

To Listen

God's love is unlimited, so there must be universal salvation. Each soul must ultimately be freed from its own individual hell and achieve heaven.

—Roy A. Burkhart

To Ponder

"Universal salvation" is the opposite of "eternal damnation," which Burkhart rejects as unbiblical. Such an unorthodox theology is worth noting, because it removes reason to fear death; also, survivors need have no negative fear of God, because their loved one will ultimately have salvation.

This theology has complete agreement from Leslie Weatherhead (*Life Begins at Death*), who says that if the Love of God is the greatest force in the universe (which he believes), then it would be a defeat for God if ultimately there was a single soul (or angel or demon) who did not respond to the pull of God's love.

Both agree that this is a strong reason why we should pray for our dead—more especially those not "saved" on earth.

To Remember

Work for the salvation of all—but don't worry about it!

To Record

May 30

To Listen

For God so loved the world that he gave his only Son, that whoever believes in him should not perish but have eternal life.

—John 3:16

To Ponder

This is the Love revealed in Christ and that can completely remake and change us in this life or in levels elsewhere. We can be made over again, reborn, as Nicodemus was to learn after his midnight interview with Christ and his discovery of the meaning of spiritual initiation. The initiation in Christ, or that experience, for instance, in the Eleusinian Mysteries, where the initiate finds the reality of eternal life in communion with Demeter and Persephone, means joyous new life. Not least among the values of the never-to-be-forgotten ecstatic vision is freedom from unwanted past influences. With this freedom there comes an awareness of another level of life in the continuing consciousness beyond this world.

To Remember

Light has come into the world; you need not choose darkness.

To Record

To Listen

I am the light of the world; he who follows me will not walk in darkness, but will have the light of life.

—John 8:12

To Ponder

When the soul awakens, there is a finding of wonderful blessings. In mystic moments we do at times have a foretaste of the glory to come. We are pilgrims here, and it is a great thing to see what awaits us there, and to know where we shall live hereafter. A Moslem mystic describes the beauty of the next world which he calls Eden, and after describing it with vivid reference to the light of the atmosphere and the shining gems of city streets, he goes on to say that a great inexpressible joy comes when one is led into the glorious realm and the veil is lifted to behold the face of Allah. This is the Beatific Vision, the ancient face of Isis shining.

To Remember

Love is the light of paradise.

To Record

CREATIVITY AND HUMAN POTENTIAL

Creativity is the process whereby something, often new, is brought into being. The creative person possesses a power, sometimes known to us as imagination, which has a potency and brings about a state of actual expression. This potency or potential often springs forth from an untapped power, an energy.

Science is now telling us what metaphysics has expressed down through the ages—that *NO THING* exists in the universe except energy. This building block of spirit and matter alike is the very source which creates what we perceive outside ourselves and generates all that is within. We draw this energy into our thought processes, and with its help, we create what we want to be the pattern for our lives. This energy knows no boundaries of space or limitations of time.

Thought proceeds from this energy and can bring matter into existence and Being. Thus, our power of creativity and human potential is only as limited as we allow it to be. With this process of materialization and actualization, we must, however, use a great deal of integrity. Constantly, we must ask ourselves if what we're doing is for the highest good, not only for ourselves but for others, many whom we know and others whom we do not know. We need always to remind ourselves that *each* person holds the same power which we possess.

We're called today to develop our own creativity through tapping into the intuitive process. As with meditation, the first step is to relax and let go of physical stress and tension. In this relaxed state we may then focus our awareness on the issue, concern or decision at hand. The third step is to be aware, open, and receptive to all forms of subjective experience, both our own and the experiences of those closely connected with us and our environment. Intuition comes to us, and the creative process opens to us through ideas, messages, expressions and images from our inner self, as we penetrate with our consciousness the invisible line between our own psyche and the outer collective psyche of the universe.

There are other ways we can add to this process of opening ourselves more fully to creativity. By affirmations we can reprogram our unconscious ideas and images—through both mental visualization and verbal repetition—with the ideas and concepts we want to accept and implement. Through studying our dreams, we can go into the unconscious and discover the nuggets of golden wisdom hidden there. Paul Brunton once said, "Once we push the gate of the mind slightly ajar and let the light stream in, the meaning of life becomes silently revealed to us."

Creative and intuitive abilities are needed today to guide society. Creative work *enlarges* the universe by adding or uncovering new dimensions. It also *enriches* and *expands* men and women through experiences both visible and invisible which are felt inwardly and which flow out of deep streams of consciousness touching into the pure source of all existence.

Truly, we are all in school here on planet Earth (perhaps while others are in school in other parts of the universe) being trained by saints and sages to understand more fully that which we need to bring into being. We're here to think reality into existence. It is an awesome challenge to our creative potential because in fact the entire planet is alive, and we can contact and work with it on the level of creative energy. We only have to remember and follow the words:

> Ask, and it will be given you; seek
> and you will find; knock, and it will
> be opened to you.
>
> Matthew 7:7

ABOUT THE AUTHOR

Kenneth Thurston Hurst is Life Member of SFF and lives near the Hudson River in New York state. He is a member of the Executive Committee and Council of SFF and is well known for his lectures, workshops, and writing in the area of the Power of the Mind and Spirit. Mr. Hurst is the President Emeritus of Prentice Hall International. He is the author of Live Life First Class, published in 1985.

—the Editor

June 1

To Listen

For with God nothing shall be impossible.

—Luke 1:37

To Ponder

Acknowledge your limitations...and they are yours. But determine to rise above them and you'll soar like an eagle! How? St. Luke tells us in straightforward language: hook up with God as your partner, and the sky is the limit! Note that Luke does not say some things...or maybe— no! He claims nothing shall be impossible. That's a tall statement. But then if your idea of God is anything like mine why shouldn't it be true? Isn't our God an *infinite* being, and my dictionary defines infinite as "Without limits, Boundless, etc." Just look up into the heavens and see the infinity of space and stars—the Power which made *that* can help *you* achieve your objectives!

To Remember

All things...not just some things...but all things are possible for me with God's help.

To Record

To Listen

Hitch your wagon to a star.

—Ralph Waldo Emerson

To Ponder

Aim for the highest, advises America's own Sage. Don't settle for second best when you can have the very BEST. There are untapped resources within you beyond the everyday self you take for granted. How reach them? The time-tested way is via meditation—which simply means going within to "the secret place of the Lord Most High." There are books galore on meditation, but they all boil down to this. Sit comfortably in a quiet spot, drain your mind of everyday worries and thoughts, concentrate upon a sacred text or emblem, and open up consciously to your Higher Self. Let it flood your being with its divine inspiration and uplift. You'll emerge refreshed and renewed!

To Remember

None but the best is good enough for the children of God—and I am a child of God!

To Record

June 3

To Listen

This very hour begin to do the work thy spirit glories in. A thousand unseen forces wait to aid. Begin!

—Paul Brunton

To Ponder

Every writer knows how difficult it is to get down to the business of writing. We sharpen our pencils and straighten our paper endlessly and seize any excuse to put off what must be done. There's a simple antidote: first offer up a prayer for guidance and inspiration and add, if possible, a short meditation to contact the Source within. Then invoke the assistance of "unseen forces waiting to aid"—and begin, begin! Whatever your creative task—writing, painting, drawing—whatever it may be, start doing something. It doesn't matter if it's good or bad, you can tear it up later, the essential point is to get the creative juices flowing. Once they've warmed up, you'll easily hit your stride.

To Remember

The only way to start any creative project is—to get started. The rest will flow.

To Record

To Listen

When we use our creative imagination in strong faith, it will create for us whatever we have formed in thought.

—Ernest Holmes

To Ponder

Visualizing an event before it happens is a valuable aid to high achievement. You can see yourself participating happily and successfully in advance. A golfer, for example, may play a winning game several times mentally before the actual match thereby gaining a far more positive outlook for the contest and programming himself mentally in advance for victory. No matter what your work may be, see yourself being successful. Take the time for positive visualization. Such mental imagery, practiced in a positive manner, builds familiarity and will boost your self-confidence. This very useful technique can help you to achieve highly!

To Remember

Today I will program myself for success by rehearsing upcoming events mentally.

To Record

June 5

To Listen

If thou canst believe, all things are possible to him that believes.

—Mark 9:23

To Ponder

Here Jesus reiterates what the angel Gabriel told his mother, Mary, that "naught shall be impossible with God." Yes, real faith works wonders. The Bible tells us we are made in the image of God. Therefore we inherit some of the infinite creative power of God. "If ye have faith but akin to a grain of mustard seed, then can ye move mountains." So whatever challenge faces us, whatever we have to do, we can best tackle it by first repeating Jesus' words. Repeat them often. Let them sink into our subconscious. Then we'll go out roaring like stouthearted lions of God...going on to victory and success!

To Remember

If I think I can, then I CAN!

To Record

To Listen

He who is happy within, who is illuminated within...becoming the Eternal, goeth to the peace of the Eternal.

—The Bhagavad Gita

To Ponder

The hidden wisdom of God is the knowledge that we are one with the Divine Being. We are really princes dreaming we are beggars. When we awake to our Divine inheritance we realize the fullness of our inner potential. This calls for the recognition of the Spirit as an indwelling Presence as well as an overshadowing Power. The road to self-discovery calls for the clearing away of the underbrush of ignorance, fear, and a sense of isolation which has made us feel we were unworthy. We need to discover our true Self and banish the bogeys of yesterday.

To Remember

The divine Spirit within me protects, guides, and directs me unerringly.

To Record

June 7

The only thing we have to fear is fear itself.
— Franklin Delano Roosevelt

To Ponder

So true! Once we stand up to that big bully Fear and grasp it round the neck and shake it, it collapses and subsides into a pile of empty rags. Yes, it's the anticipation of the event, not the event itself, that causes us to quake in our boots and fear the worst. Fear festers best at 3 A.M. as we lie helpless in our beds: comes the dawn, however, and we are too busy to entertain this unwelcome guest. So, the key to banishing fear is *action*. "Do the thing we fear, and the death of fear is certain!! said Emerson.

To Remember

Today I will fear naught, for nothing ever turns out as bad as fear paints it.

To Record

To Listen

Every day, in every way, I'm getting better and better.

—Emile Coue

To Ponder

The power of auto-suggestion. That which sends messages to our subconscious. Oft repeated, they can materialize in our lives. So be careful not to complain "that person gives me a pain in the neck!"—or that's just what you might get. Rather use positive affirmations like the one quoted above. Use them daily until they sink firmly into your subconscious. Make up your own to fit your personal needs and goals. Think of them as mental vitamins; take them every morning before you face the world. You'll be glad you did!

To Remember

Today I radiate good health, enjoy pleasant feelings, and expect the best life can offer!

To Record

June 9

To Listen

Since wars begin in the minds of men, it is in the minds of men that the defenses of peace must be constructed.

—United Nations Charter

To Ponder

In other words, while we think aggressive thoughts of hatred, we are sowing the seeds for their outer manifestation in the form of wars. If man can't live at peace with his neighbor and quarrels over a borrowed lawnmower or boundary fence, what hope is there for nations to behave differently? Because nations are but collections of individuals, after all. So charity begins at home, as St. Paul declared, and our personal charity toward others can count in the scale. Thoughts of peace, of charity and yes, of love do count. They are like candles in a dark room; enough of them and they disperse the surrounding darkness.

To Remember

Today I will project only loving thoughts to the world and to every person I meet.

To Record

To Listen

The world is too much with us; late and soon, getting and spending, we lay waste to our powers.

—William Wordsworth

To Ponder

In the frenetic pace of our busy lives, amid the hustle and bustle of making a living, it's easy to overlook the real purpose of our lives here on earth. We forget that what really counts, all that we can take with us, is the inner development of our spiritual character. So from time to time it's necessary to take a break from everyday routine and be by ourselves or with like-minded friends to devote ourselves to matters of the spirit. Put our computers on one side, forego the counting house and turn our faces toward asking "What's life all about?" "Why was I born?" "What's the meaning of it all?" Thus we start storing up eternal riches in heaven.

To Remember

Today I will take time out to give myself a "spirit break" to renew myself.

To Record

June 11

To Listen

I will instruct thee and teach thee in the way which thou shalt go; I will guide thee with mine eye.

—Psalm 32:8

To Ponder

We need plans and goals in life so we do not drift aimlessly. But what guides us in choosing our direction? If we rely solely on our human intellect, we can easily make mistakes. However, when we turn to the Infinite Intuition within, then we are Divinely guided, as the psalmist promised. Just as the swallows are guided to return thousands of miles annually to Capistrano. How do we obtain such guidance? Through prayer, through meditation, through consciously offering up our lives to the Higher Power to be used as It wishes. "Let not my will but Thy will be done."

To Remember

Today and every day, my Inner Guidance directs me in all my activities.

To Record

To Listen

Before they call, I will answer.

—Isaiah 65:24

To Ponder

A teacher has said "Be careful what you pray for because you will get it." Your spoken and written words have power. Even your thoughts, imbued with energy, have power. This is because we are made in the image of our Creator—and therefore possess some of Its creativity. So be careful when you pray, be specific about *what* you want yet let the Higher Power decide *how* you are to get it. Instead of praying to be a millionaire, for instance (currency could quickly lose value in a period of rapid inflation) affirm that God provides for *all* your financial needs.

To Remember

I pray that I shall receive from the universe that which is best for me.

To Record

June 13

To Listen

Ye are the light of the world.

—Matthew 5:14

To Ponder

Let's not underrate ourselves. For we have the most important, the most powerful Parent in the universe. And what parent doesn't wish the very best for its children? Yes, we have a fantastic birthright if only we knew how to reach out and grasp it. So why settle for less than the best? Posit what we want in clear bright colors, aim for the very finest in every area of our being. Give it everything you've got—and see how Life reflects it back to you. You deserve the best. Claim your celestial birthright. Dare to be all that you have it within you to be!

To Remember

Today I expect only the very best in every sphere of my activities.

To Record

To Listen

We have met the enemy and they is us.

—Pogo

To Ponder

You are a child of God. And so is everyone else. Today, when you meet your loved ones, your fellow workers, shoppers in the supermarket or people in the street, the beggar on the corner, look at them and treat them as if you were interacting with God Itself—because you are. "Namaste!" is the hallowed Hindu greeting meaning "I salute the Divinity within you." "I worship thee, not for thee alone but for Heaven which hangs over thee" wrote the poet Robert Browning to his wife. Practice this daily...and you'll start to see people in a new light, for we are all closely bound by a spiritual kinship.

To Remember

Today I direct love and friendship to all humanity.

To Record

June 15

To Listen

We live, move, and have our being in God. . . . For we are also his offspring.

—Acts 17:28

To Ponder

Yesterday we realized that we are all one, related through God. Today we can go a step further and confirm that nothing else exists but God. We are like fish, swimming in water and asking, "Is there such a thing as water?" So to the question "How does one find God—well, one doesn't, because God was never lost! God is here all the time, in everything we see and experience. What a wonderful revelation! To know that we exist in the body of God—just as millions of cells live within our body. And as long as we keep in harmony within our Divine structure, no ill can befall us. For then we truly live in the light.

To Remember

Today I walk in the light and spread the light to all I meet.

To Record

To Listen

The kingdom of heaven is like a merchant who when he found one great pearl, sold all he had and sought it.

—Matthew 13:45-46

To Ponder

There is a great pearl deep within each of us. A pearl, truly priceless, worth more than all our other possessions. A pearl that is a magic talisman possessed of incredible power. You've probably read the story of the prospector who unsucessfully scoured the world for diamonds, finally gave up and returned home only to find them in his own backyard. So instead of looking outwards for our happiness we would be better off exploring within via daily meditation, opening ourselves to the Sacred Presence and entering Its hallowed precincts.

To Remember

I will no longer seek outward for my good, for I know that it cometh from within.

To Record

June 17

To Listen

It is only with the heart that one can see rightly; what is essential is invisible to the eye.

—Antoine de Saint-Exupery

To Ponder

Yes, the greatest things in life are invisible. St. Paul listed them as faith, hope and charity— and the greatest of these is charity, he said. Today we would translate the Greek word *agape* as love, rather than charity—and we'd be closer to the mark. Love is the greatest power in the world. Love springs from the heart. "Love is kind, love is gentle, love suffereth much," said St. Paul. The power of love can even transcend the grave. The great values, the eternal verities, all have their roots in the heart. All else is non-essential despite the clamor it may make for our attention.

To Remember

I concentrate upon those lessons of the heart— the great lessons of love, faith, and hope.

To Record

To Listen
That's one small step for a man, one giant leap for mankind.

—Neil Armstrong

To Ponder
We may be on the threshold of exploring outer space but the real challenge remains that of inner space. We have barely tapped exploring our inner potential. We take for granted our standard I.Q. measurements. But how much more are we really capable of? Not from our own limited brain power but utilizing the unfathomable resources of Mind—that universal Mind present in all of us. By invoking its aid and harnessing its strength we can find ourselves possessed of inspiration undreamt of. And the key to this mental treasure-trove lies within—to be reached by regular meditation.

To Remember
I become aware of a Power within me that guides me and inspires me.

To Record

June 19

To Listen

You will find rest from vain fancies if you perform every act in life as though it were your last.

—Marcus Aurelius

To Ponder

There's a current saying: "Today is the first day of the rest of your life." If we could but live in the Now, savor each passing moment to the full, how much richer our lives would be! Too often we let time slip by rueing yesterday's disappointments or dreaming of future imaginary delights. Only the Now is real. This very minute contains all the essence of Life—it is all we have to deal with right now! Let us give it our undivided attention and concentrate upon what we are doing. We will enjoy it that much more and do it better than we could otherwise.

To Remember

Today I will fill each minute with sixty seconds worth of value.

To Record

To Listen

Hope is the beautiful message of the unknown goal, the encouragement of the sublime perfect to the struggling imperfect.

—Paul Brunton

To Ponder

Just as all of us on the spiritual quest are actively seeking God, although we can't go so far as to say that God is seeking us, nevertheless we can avow that God is actively attracting us to Itself, just as a magnet attracts iron filings. We might even go further and acknowledge that God takes an interest in us and our spiritual progress. As Emerson declared, "Man's welfare is dear to the heart of Being." And God has planted the lovely flower of Hope in us that we might know we are never left alone, that we are never deserted, and that there is light at the end of the tunnel of the dark night of the Soul.

To Remember

I know that I can reach out and entrust my hand to the hand of God.

To Record

June 21

To Listen

I am come that they might have life, and that they might have it more abundantly.

—John 10:10

To Ponder

How many people just drift through life, only half-alive, utilizing but a fraction of their potential! Buffeted by the winds of fate they make little or no attempt to control their destinies. "What can you do?" they complain. Well, we can do a lot. Because God has given us the priceless boon of *choice*. In effect, we can choose to be happy or unhappy. Because whatever happens to us is not as important as our *reaction* to what happened. "Naught is good nor bad but thinking makes it so" wrote Shakespeare. So make it your choice to be on the positive side of life...determine to enjoy to the fullest life's many blessings.

To Remember

The universe showers abundant life upon me. I accept it today and every day.

To Record

To Listen

For God hath not given us the spirit of fear; but of power, and of love, and of a sound mind.
—II Timothy 1:7

To Ponder

So let us claim our birthright, the gifts our Creator has for us...power, love and a sound mind. What fantastic presents! What more could we wish for! Take each word and meditate upon it in turn. Let the full meaning soak into your subconscious. Drop all fear out of your mind; replace it with power and love—and your mind will be sound again. And you will experience fresh, vital energy.

To Remember

I accept God's gifts of power and love—and I reflect them to all I meet.

To Record

June 23

To Listen

And a man's foes shall be the they of his own household.

—Matthew 10:36

To Ponder

Yes, we create our own problems. The fears and worries and hostilities we carry within ourselves are projected into the outer world. And they boomerang right back at us. Most people are like passengers on a train who insist on carrying their suitcases instead of putting them down and letting the train itself carry them. The basic lesson of the Universe is to cease relying upon our little selves and to commit ourselves to that Greater Self, to turn over our problems to It—to let go and let God. It is ever-ready to take over and assist us. "For behold I stand at the door and knock."

To Remember

Today I will trust in the Lord and walk in step with him.

To Record

To Listen

And all things, whatsoever ye shall ask in prayer, believing, ye shall receive.

—Matthew 21:22

To Ponder

The key word is *believing*. Just to mumble rote phrases is not enough. Nor did Jesus refer to our belief in any creed or theology, but rather the firm belief that what we have asked for in prayer is already established. It may take time to materialize on the outer plane, but the seed has been planted. It takes time for the flower to grow, but grow it will. For our part we need patience and faith, the firm faith of expectancy that our need is being satisfied.

To Remember

I give thanks now that my need is being met at the right time.

To Record

To Listen

This is the day the Lord hath made; let us rejoice and be glad in it.

—Psalm 117:24

To Ponder

What a stirring affirmation with which to start the morning! The first few minutes upon awakening are fraught with potential for programming the kind of day we are going to have. Let's take advantage of a clear mind to fill it with thoughts of God, of happiness, of health, of prosperity. While we shower and dress, let us follow the *command* of the psalmist and REJOICE! Then when we leave our home and head for the office we'll hit the ground running primed to have a great day.

To Remember

Today I'm going to have a great day in every way!

To Record

To Listen

And be renewed in the spirit of your mind.
—Ephesians 4:23

To Ponder

Each new day offers us the opportunity to be RE-NEWED. Each dawn is a new deal...a brand new clean slate. Our yesterdays are washed away, and we have a fresh beginning. Today you can be the person you want to be; you can put your best look forward and go whistling through the day. Don't let yesterday's shadows affect you; today you are the new YOU, a new person—today is the first day of the rest of your life!

To Remember

Today I will show forth my best self to everyone I meet.

To Record

June 27

To Listen

Neglect not the gift that is in thee.

—I Timothy 4:14

To Ponder

What is this gift within us? It certainly ties in with this month's theme of exploring our inner potential. For within us is the Indwelling Presence which mystics have tried to describe throughout the ages. So St. Paul is advising us not to overlook this priceless pearl buried deep within us as we become engrossed in the business of making a living in the outside world. We need to balance the two, and the gift within us will help us cope with the outer—and all the more effectively.

To Remember

I turn to the power of God within me and accept it in my life.

To Record

To Listen

He revealeth the deep and sacred things; he knoweth what is in the darkness.

—Daniel 2:22

To Ponder

The greatest treasures are always the most carefully hidden. Deep within us is the key to unlocking our fullest potential. By going within and making contact with the source of all Power, we can transform our outer lives. A regular program of meditation—thirty minutes daily in quiet surroundings—will enable us to make the God connection. Thus we can tap Its unlimited wisdom and strength to guide and sustain us in daily living. After all, if we cannot find time for God, how can we expect God to find time for us?

To Remember

I will find time to commune with God today and every day.

To Record

June 29

To Listen

Man's extremity is God's opportunity.

—Paul Brunton

To Ponder

When our lives flow smoothly we tend to take God for granted. But when problems arise and we find that our human resources are too limited to cope with the situation, that is when we turn to God and pray for help. And God is always there. "Come unto me all who are heavy laden and I will give them rest." So seeming bad news can turn out to be good news if we have reestablished our God connection and are once again in tune with our Higher Power through prayer and meditation.

To Remember

I will hold onto my lifeline with my higher self and commune with it daily.

To Record

To Listen

The greatest discovery of my generation is that human beings can alter their lives by altering their attitudes of mind.

—William James

To Ponder

Here creativity and exploring our hidden potential merge to form this tremendous statement—that we can change our circumstances by changing our thought patterns. Yes, if we don't like the menu life is presenting to us right now, we can order something else just by mentally setting the wheels into motion. How? By deciding exactly what we do want, spelling it out clearly, and affirming with fervor that we already possess it. Thus we draw it into our lives through the power of the law of attraction.

To Remember

I can transform my life for the better by how I think today.

To Record

Artist: Jan Spencer,
St. Paul, Minnesota

INTERDEPENDENCE AND RELATIONSHIPS

The secret of all meaningful relationships lies not in either independence or dependence but rather in relating interdependently with others. Our interdependency is the cornerstone of our connectedness with each other on a spiritual level. Because of the inseparable and indivisible bond of eternal oneness which exists, we, in order to live in harmony and love, are called to make a connection in which we are mutually interdependent. To relate literally means to be carried back and to recognize a connection. This connection was made at the beginning of the evolutionary process of the existence of *life* when the worlds were "called into Being."

The love which we show to others is the result of identifying our inner connection with God, and thus with everyone else. If we truly love our neighbor, we do not play favorites or claim special privileges. One of the most important contributions we can make to the political, social and economic issues we face today is to recognize honestly that we all need each other to bring about a universal state of peace. We are all inescapably connected, and in no way can any one of us have or know complete love until we all know complete love.

One of the greatest challenges we face in relationships is being able to give freely with no thought of what we may receive. When we expect a reward, or some particular recognition for our gifts or service, we are violating the spiritual law of the universe which demands from us an outpouring that seeks no reward and asks no return. The secret, however, is that what you give ultimately will return to you.

This month, as we contemplate our interdependence in relationships, we will begin with our own relationship to the spirit within, by which we recognize our divine reality and the potential for expressing divine qualities in the world around us. John Rossner, the author for this month's reflections, has gathered his citations from "Ancient Wisdom Traditions of East and West, and texts from the Christian

New Testament, the Hebrew Psalms of David (*Psalms Now*, translations by Leslie F. Brandt, Concordia, 1973), Indian Yoga and Vedanta Philosophy, the Hermetica (ancient Greek and Latin writings which contain religious or philosophic teachings attributed to Hermes Trismegistus)," the 1940 Hymnal, and *The Primordial Tradition*—his own work.

When we can look another person in the eye and know we can trust them, we will connect with our corporate roots, know a sense of permanent peace, and feel a sense of absolute completeness. At that moment, we experience our soul mirrored in the eyes we behold, and we know there is only one family of humanity. When we are separated from this one source, we are incomplete, but when we are joined, we find our point of peace and wholeness. Only when we are joined will we fully understand:

> I in them and thou in me,
> that they may become perfectly
> one, so that the world may
> know that thou hast sent me and
> hast loved them even as thou
> hast loved me.
>
> John 17:23

ABOUT THE AUTHOR

John Leslie Rossner is on the faculty of Concordia University in Montreal, Canada, and is an Anglican priest. He has been active in SFF as a lecturer and workshop leader and is on the Executive Committee and Council as Vice President. He is a world traveler and the author of a five-volume series on the Primordial Tradition. He lives with his wife Marilyn in Montreal.

—the Editor

To Listen

We must awaken to the reality of the Spirit within...in order to realize social maturity and harmony in the world without.

—John Rossner

To Ponder

True mystics everywhere—East and West, ancient and modern—have always known that there can be no peace on earth, no real social justice, and no perfection in the outer-order of things in the world...until enough human beings awaken to the reality of the highest, most authentic levels of the Self within.

This authentic Self has been described in various Wisdom traditions as "Imago Dei" (Latin Christianity), the "Ruach Adonai" (Hebrew Bible), the "Atman" (Sanscrit Hindu Scriptures), or "the Light which lightens everyman who comes into the world" (the Fourth Gospel and Gnostic traditions).

To Remember

I must look within and seek the flame of the Spirit in order to cleanse the inner vessel, find my truest self, and create a better world.

To Record

July 2

To Listen

I and the Father are one; I am in him and he is in me. . .I dwell in you, and you in me. . .I am the vine and you are the branches.

—John 10:30 & 38; 15:5

To Ponder

That Spirit, that "Atman," that "Image of God" in you is the core of your own authentic being. Yet it is only rarely experienced by most people who dwell in ordinary, or mundane states of consciousness most of their lives.

Great saints and mystics, however, have told us about it after they have learned to dwell in, and operate out of such "Superconscious" levels of mind in which they have contacted the Spirit.

In ancient Sanscrit texts, the Superconscious level of mind was called the "buddhi," and anyone who lived in it was called a "buddha." Similarily, in the Judeo-Christian tradition, one who was "anointed" by the Spirit of God was called "an anointed one." In Hebrew "an anointed one" is "a messiah"; and, in Greek this is translated as "a christ."

To Remember

My goal is to know the authentic core of my own being, the "pure formless Spirit."

To Record

To Listen

Behold, I stand at the door and knock; and, if any man open I will come in and sup with him.
—Revelation 3:20

To Ponder

The Eternal Christ—whose Image and Breath already form the most authentic, inner core of your being—"stands at the door" of your earthly heart and mind, and seeks entry.

Lo, He is "out there"—as if another person on the Path—but He is more than that! He is also already "in here," in your innermost being and mind.

He is the archetype, or blueprint, of the God-like, higher, truest Self in you. And yet He stands "out there," beyond "the door" of your ego, humbly seeking permission of that "nothing little self" to come in, take up His rightful abode in your body, soul, and mind to "feast with you" on the spiritual riches at the Heavenly Father's table: Love, Joy, Peace, Forgiveness, Self-less Service of all God's children.

To Remember

Lord, I hear you knocking at the door of my heart. I would cleanse my house and bid you enter.

To Record

July 4

To Listen

In order to see God, a man must first cleanse and empty himself, and stand outside of himself.

—St. Gregory Palamas

To Ponder

In order to know inwardly that God exists and is reflected in our highest and truest Self, we must first be cleansed of all negative thought patterns and behaviors, and stand outside of, apart from, the egoic or lower levels of our being.

Saints and mystics of East & West—like the yogis and rishis of India—have caught rare and precious glimpses of this truest Self in the highest moments of consciousness...and proclaimed that God is present in It, and that It is present in every living person. From such "peak experiences" they have gone on to live lives of compassion, love, and self-less service for all humanity.

To Remember

I must look within and seek the flame of the Spirit, in order to cleanse the inner vessel, find my truest self, and create a better world.

To Record

To Listen

I am not the body; I am not the mind; I am Sat,
Chit, Ananda (Pure Existence, Pure Conscious-
ness, Pure Bliss)

—The Yogi after Meditation

To Ponder

When we are in the state of Supreme Awareness we know that we are not just a body, not
just the mental processes, but that we are first
and foremost "sparks of the Divine," or "sons"
and "daughters" of God.

At the same time we also know that "sparks
of the same Divine Reality" also form the innermost core of the beings of all of our neighbors
in the human race, and indeed, in varying
degrees, of all living creatures.

We know them somehow to be "one with us,"
and "we with them."

For persons who have achieved such a state
of awareness it becomes inconceivable that
anything should be done which might hurt, or
inflict suffering on any other living creature.

To Remember

I will strive to attain the Highest State of Con-
sciousness. . .that I might live my entire life on
the "Rock" of divine love toward all.

To Record

July 6

To Listen

Not I, but the Christ who lives within me, enables me to do all things.

—I Corinthians 15:10

To Ponder

Only as a person is "awakened" to the reality of this highest level of the Self within, or this "Light which lightens everyman who comes into the world," can he or she experience the peace, the enlightened vision, and the higher conscousness which are the signs of its Presence.

Only when the awareness of this highest level of the Self dawns will one open the doors of the heart to the eternal God-Man and invite Him to enter in and begin the process of our transformation into new beings.

Only then will we find the motivation, the power, and the inner strength to change ethically into the kind of new being who is really sensitive to the sufferings and joys, the needs and the rights of others. . . in our world of interdependence and relationships.

To Remember

I must look within and seek the flame of the Spirit, in order to cleanse the inner vessel, find my truest self, and create a better world.

To Record

To Listen

*Let those who have eyes, see; and let those who
have ears to hear, hear!*

—Ezekiel 12:2, Matthew 11:15

To Ponder

It is only those who are "awakened" to the
reality of the Spirit within who can see our true
human condition, or "hear the still, small
voice" of God in conscience.

Thus awakened to the spiritual and moral significance of the issues around us—otherwise
veiled from us—we suddenly must become
ethical beings, must become "our brother's
keeper."

Only then will we—like the saints of all traditions—want to lead a life of ego-less service.
And only then will we be really "safe and
reliable" human beings.

Only then will there be a sufficiently trustworthy and emotionally balanced human
species on this planet capable of controlling
our sciences, technologies, economies, and our
political or social structures...according to the
highest standards and our fullest human potential.

To Remember

*I will seek after the Spirit of God...that I might
take part in bringing a "new heaven and a new
earth" to our planet.*

To Record

July 8

To Listen

In order to enter the kingdom of heaven, you must be born again.

—John 3:5

To Ponder

Our interdependence and relationships in the outer-world can not, and will not function as they should—according to the Divine Blueprint—until we have been awakened and changed, or "born again" into the new, and highest state of spiritual and ethical consciousness.

This process depends upon our openness to receive the action of the living Spirit of God within our hearts and souls...to cleanse, forgive, heal, and "raise-up" that Divine Image which—although obscured by a lifetime of neglect—is our birthright.

Thus our world-without depends for its health and well-being upon our world-within, both individually and collectively as the human race. It is because of this metaphysical fact, that the saints have recognized that all worth-while and lasting social reform depends ultimately upon inner, psychospiritual transformation in the citizenry of a given place or time.

To Remember

I must look within and seek the flame of the Spirit, in order to cleanse the inner vessel, find my truest self, and create a better world.

To Record

To Listen

*In your general discourses, father... you said
that no one can be saved until he has been born
again; but you did not make known to me what
you meant by this.*

—Hermes Trismegistus

To Ponder

HERMES: "If you would be born again, you
must cleanse yourself from the irrational torments."

HIS SON: "What, father, have I torturers
within me?"

HERMES: "Yes, my son, and not a few; they
are terrible, and they are many."

HIS SON: "I do not know them, father."

HERMES: "This very Ignorance, my son, is
one of the torments. The second is Grief. The
third is Incontinence. The fourth is Desire. The
fifth is Injustice. The sixth is Covetousness. The
seventh is Deceitfulness. The eighth is Envy.
The ninth is Fraud. The tenth is Anger. The
eleventh is Rashness. The twelfth is Vice. These
are twelve in number; and under them there are
many others also, my son."

To Remember

*In order to be "born again" into higher con-
sciousness, I will cleanse myself and my relationships by seeking to eliminate these twelve deadly
"torturers."*

To Record

July 10

To Listen

Rejoice now, my son; you are being cleansed by the powers of God; for they have come to build up in you the body of reason.

> —Hermes Trismegistus

To Ponder

"The knowledge of God has come to us; and at its coming, my son, Ignorance has been driven out. Joy has come to us; and at her coming, my son, Grief will flee away to enter those in whom there is room for her."

The only way to exorcize the twelve deadly "tormentors" is to invite into our hearts and lives the ten "Powers of God" (The "Holy Decad").

Thus Ignorance will flee when the inner Knowledge of God enters; and Grief or pessimism and depression must leave us whenever we invite Joy into our lives by allowing ourselves to find it everywhere...in the sunlight, in the rain, in the sky, in the sea, in the earth, in the ability to perform our daily tasks, in our food, in our rest, in the faces of our friends, in strangers...everywhere if we look with the right eyes.

To Remember

I invite the inner knowledge of God and the spirit of joy into my innermost being.

To Record

To Listen

And after Joy, I summon a third Power, even Continence, O sweetest Power! Let us receive her, my son, most gladly.

—Hermes Trismegistus

To Ponder

"See how, at the instant of her coming, she has pushed Incontinence away."

Continence is the essence of contentedness, the sign of inner fullness and self-satisfaction in God. Rather than the empty craving or yearning that comes from a sense of incompleteness or lacking, one is content, satisfied, and happy with the gifts that God and Nature have already given.

Thus, with incontinence, lust, craving after anything, one can not be truly happy, or at peace, Only Continence is the sign of fulfillment, and the absence of any sense of lacking. Some people, no matter how much they have of wealth or emotional gratification are still restless...incontinent! No relationships can survive in an incontinent, restless soul.

To Remember

I will seek the divine power of Continence, to drive away all discontent...and to establish my relationships on the rock of spiritual fulfillment.

To Record

July 12

To Listen

And now I summon a fourth Power, Endurance...the opposite of Desire.

—Hermes Trismegistus

To Ponder

Without Endurance—stick-to-it-iveness, patient discipline to finish our highest and good resolutions—both our spiritual and material lives will fail, and we will be left only with an empty bag of unfulfilled dreams, empty desires and a resentful craving for that which we might have accomplished.

Thus Endurance is necessary to the fulfillment of the Divine Plan for us which Higher Consciousness reveals in those creative, intuitive flashes of inspiration and guidance. But Endurance is our part of the deal, the proper human response to God's Revelation of a new and better way.

The summoning of the Divine Power of Endurance is necessary to keep us on the Path in those difficult moments when others challenge us and tempt us to compromise our vision and our values.

To Remember

I will pray daily for the divine power of Endurance, and remember my life's spiritual purpose in all that I do.

To Record

To Listen
And this, my son, is the tribunal upon which Justice sits enthroned.

—Hermes Trismegistus

To Ponder
"See how she has driven out Injustice! When we have been justified, my son, we are not brought to Judgment; for Injustice is no longer there."

Justice in our interrelations and relationships is absolutely essential to our own peace and prosperity—both as individuals and as nations. But alas, neither the human race nor its nations have yet learned this primary, most basic lesson!

Thus it is hard for us—as individuals who would walk the universal Spiritual Path—to find models or reinforcement for our efforts to be pure, unselfish, and just in all of our dealings with others.

Yet the Spirit and Power of Justice—whenever sincerely summoned—will come surely and swiftly to dethrone Injustice in all of our resolutions.

To Remember
Come, O mighty power of Justice, inspire and cleanse my heart, and that of my people.

To Record

July 14

To Listen

As the sixth Power, I call to us Unselfishness, the opponent of Covetousness. And when Covetousness has departed...Unselfishness will reign.

—Hermes Trismegistus

To Ponder

In all of the great World Religions, East and West, Selfishness, or an egoic me-first attitude, is seen as the principal human vice.

In the Judeo-Christian tradition, it is the reason that Cain slew Abel, and Jesus reminds us that..."whosoever loses himself for my sake, will find himself." Egotism and self-centered grasping is always at the expense of others, including God.

Yet, we can invoke the Spirit and Power of Unselfishness into our lives and beings if we really want to! Think of the greatest saints...think of Mother Theresa every morning when you wake up. She will have been up for hours, pushing a cart through the streets of Calcutta looking for dying persons and abandoned children to minister to.

To Remember

Please, O Spirit of God, give me your most precious of all gifts—Unselfishness, expressed in selfless service to others.

To Record

To Listen

Unselfishness, the opponent of Covetousness.
                    —Hermetica (Libellus XII)

To Ponder

To be at the "Spiritual Frontier" we must be, first and foremost, Unselfish, not self-centered, not egotistical.

And to avoid selfishness is to renounce Covetousness.

That means that whenever someone else I know has attained something I admire or want, that I will not be jealous or envious of him or her, and that I will not covet whatever it is.

To resent someone subconsciously for their good fortune, or achievement and skill is the first sign that the mortal sins of Envy and Covetousness have taken over my heart, and that I am derailed from a sincere Spiritual Path.

The Unselfish person—like God—truly rejoices in whatever Good befalls another, simply because he or she has learned to love that other person as oneself.

To Remember

O God, give me a truly unselfish heart, that I may rejoice in the good fortune of all your creatures because I love them.

To Record

To Listen

As the seventh, I invoke Truth. Flee away, Deceit, for Truth has come.

—Hermes Trismegistus

To Ponder

Truth is not this or that static proposition to be grasped by the logical mind as a dogma. Truth is a living Spirit and a Power. Whenever we attune ourselves to it—as to the Tao, to the mystical Torah, to the Dharma, or to the Holy Spirit of God itself—we are in contact with, and enlightened by, the most awesome Living Power in the Universe!

Thus, we can not manipulate Truth or distort it to our own ends. Yet how often do we presume to limit and control truth by our own myopic standards!

This mortal sin has caused religious and ideological wars among nations, self-righteousness, and tragic, broken relationships between individuals, and within groups everywhere.

To Remember

When the living truth—which is found in the Spirit of God—comes into my life I must find humility.

To Record

To Listen

See, my son, how on the coming of Truth, the Good is completed; for Envy has departed from us, and the other torments also.

—Hermes Trismegistus

To Ponder

The Metaphysical Laws that govern the Universe are Living Intelligences—higher beings than our puny intellects. They can not be grasped by our logical minds alone, but first must be received and welcomed by our higher intuition, and only then examined feebly by our limited rational faculties.

The great Wisdom Traditions of the world have known this fact. Modern sciences and theologies have not often appreciated it.

Thus the "coming of the Truth" that our Hermetic dialogue for today describes is a momentous event: the welcoming of the Supreme Good into the humble abode of our human souls. We can experience this anytime that we are ready. The Holy Spirit of God is the Living Truth behind all the Metaphysical Laws and Principles that govern life.

To Remember

When the Holy Spirit of God comes to dwell in us, there is nothing left in the whole universe to want!

To Record

To Listen

Truth has come upon us, and on it has followed the Good with Life and Light. No longer has there come upon us any of the torments of darkness; they have flown away with rushing wings.
—Hermes Trismegistus

To Ponder

The Holy Spirit—which is the Spirit of God, Truth, Life, and Light—drives out all torment and darkness from the human psyche, and from the collective social orders of mankind.

The ancient truth behind Exorcism of Demons in all traditions is just this: "Where the finger of God is, there the Devil flees."

Thus in order to expel an evil condition—whether a spiritual, psychological, or social negative-force, we must simply flood the situation with the opposite: the Good, Life, and Light.

This was the meaning of the wise dicta which so few people on this planet have understood or practiced: "Overcome darkness with the Light; Overcome hatred with Love"...and Jesus' commandment to "forgive your enemies; love them that persecute you."

To Remember

Until I learn to forgive my enemies, to overcome hatred with love, I will have not discovered the Truth, the Good, or the Light!

To Record

To Listen

Thus, my son, has the intellectual being been made up in us and, by its coming to be, we have been made gods.

—Hermes Trismegistus

To Ponder

Jesus one day said to his disciples—quoting one of the ancient Psalms of David, "Know ye not that ye are gods."

All of the authentic Mystery and Wisdom traditions of antiquity proclaimed to their initiates: "Ye are gods in the making." And the way that we are made into gods, or transformed from mortals into immortals, was said to be by the gradual—or sudden—replacement of the vices by the virtues, or sanctification, after being "awakened" from our lethargic slumber, and "born again" as "new beings" with a new and higher consciousness.

The "fruits of the Spirit"—Love, Joy, Peace, Patience, Forgiveness, Humility, and Self-less Service to all—were the infallible signs that the Divine transformative process was complete in a man, woman or child.

To Remember

Come, O Holy Spirit, cleanse me of all vice, endow me with all virtues, that I may inherit the promise of sharing in your divinity.

To Record

To Listen

Among those, then, who dwell in that world above there is no disagreement....The spell which binds them one to another is Love...and by it all are wrought together into one harmonious whole.

—Ascelpius (Hermetica)

To Ponder

According to the ancient Wisdom traditions—and to Jesus in the New Testament, the angels and saints in the heavenly spheres "...do always behold their Father's face and do His will."

And the earth-plane on which we dwell is supposed to be the reproduction here below of the heavenly spheres, which are intended as the authentic "Blueprint" for our world.

But the "Fall of Man" from his primordial state has, rather, turned our world more often into a reflection of a hell, purgatory, or the lower astral plane.

Jesus' commandment to us for dealing with the social order is: "Thy Kingdom come, Thy will be done on the earth-plane as it already is in the heavenly places."

To Remember

The Lord's Prayer, prayed with understanding and power, brings the kingdom of God into our lives.

To Record

To Listen

He who alone has not come into being cannot be presented through sense. But if you have power to see with the eyes of the [Higher] Mind...he will manifest himself to you.

—Hermes Trismegistus

To Ponder

In our Materialistic and Rationalistic culture many people refuse to accept as real anything that they can not see with the physical eyes and logically analyze.

But in Ancient Wisdom traditions—from the Vedanta to Plato and early Christian mysticism—the "Real" world of God, heavenly beings, and the human soul itself could not be perceived by such "lower faculties" as sense perception and mechanistic logic.

For the recognition of the Divine spiritual Realities all around and in us—it was said that a process of spiritual and psychic growth and unfoldment was first required.

Perhaps this is why so many persons today, who are otherwise highly developed, have not been able to affirm the existence of God, the human soul, or the interconnectedness of all-life in any agreed-upon spiritual dimension.

To Remember

Open the eyes of my mind and of my heart, O Lord, that I may behold thee in all thy works.

To Record

July 22

To Listen

We, having received into our souls—which are of heavenly origin—the efflux of God's wisdom, must, in return, use in his service all that springs up in us.

—Hermes Trismegistus

To Ponder

All the good that we can do is but the flowering of the Divine grace and wisdom flowing through us from a heavenly Source.

Thus we can take no credit to our own egos as if they were the causes or the intelligences behind our good deeds, creative insights, or accomplishments.

All the ego can properly do is to get out of the way and not block or distort our highest and most noble impulses. And IF an ego is healthy enough to do that, it will be so humble and self-effacing that it will neither need or want to be boastful or self-congratulatory.

To Remember

O God, give me a healthy ego, so that I may use it unself-consciously in thy service.

To Record

To Listen

For those who minister and heal.
And spend themselves, their skill, their zeal;
Renew their hearts with Christ-like faith,
And guard them from disease and death;
And in thine own good time, Lord, send
Thy peace on earth till time shall end.

—John Oxenham

To Ponder

It is those who spend their lives in self-less service, ministering to the needs of the poor, the desperate, the confused, the helpless, and working to heal the sick—whether in body, soul, or spirit—who have a perfect right to expect a renewal of Christ-like faith, preservation from disease and untimely death, and the gift of inner-peace.

It is such inner spiritual peace, healing, and Christ-like faith which alone will bring true and lasting peace to planet earth.

It is that very same inner-spiritual peace, healing, and renewal which I seek at the deepest levels of myself whenever I pray or meditate, and in my entire life's quest.

To Remember

I must think of ways to spend more of my life in the selfless service to others.

To Record

To Listen

For those who weak and broken lie
In weariness and agony,
Great Healer, to their beds of pain
Come, touch and make them whole again.
O hear a people's prayers, and bless
Thy servants in their hour of stress

—John Oxenham

To Ponder

All over the world today we hear of or see people who are weak and broken, distressed and—in many cases in agony.

Because we are spiritually awakened human beings we know our interconnectedness with them, and that they too are children of the same Heavenly Father, that the same Eternal Christ dwells in them as..."the Light that lightens everyman who comes into the world."

Thus, whether seen in the daily news as victims of starvation, disease, poverty, warfare, repressive regimes abroad—or seen in the doorsteps or over the grates in the streets of our own cities—these people are our responsibility too, and that we can not wash our hands of them with some sort of cheap casuistry or self-exonerating argument.

To Remember

I vow to help those in need, either directly or through organizations set up to serve them.

To Record

To Listen

I know, O God, that you are grieved
by the selfishness of your children.
The world you created seems to be falling apart.
Your creatures are living for themselves alone.
—Psalm 5 (Modern translation)

To Ponder

As we look at the daily television news or read the newspapers we see paraded before our consciousness the portrait of a disturbed and broken human race.

It is clearly disturbed by selfishness, egotism, and the Seven Deadly Sins—including Anger, Lust, Covetousness, Envy. This has led to an orgy of warfare, crime, injustice, terrorism, and insensitivity to human suffering.

And yet there is Hope. That Hope resides in your Compassion and mine...but above all in God's Compassion, which is made known in and through ours. And that Compassion can only be expressed through acts of Selfless Love rendered in His Name as an example and a remedy for the Sin of the World.

To Remember

Give me the courage and the spirit of selfless service and love, O Lord, which is your divine remedy.

To Record

To Listen

*The philosophies that come out of our world
bear little resemblance
to the truth you revealed to us....
Enable us to recognize them for what they are.*
                    —Psalm 5 (Modern translation)

To Ponder

The false worldly philosophies that the Psalmist describes are numerous, and should be all too familiar to us. Among them are:

Take whatever you can get in life. It's the other fellow's problem if he gets in my way, or that of my company, country, etc. I just call this developing my human potential.

If someone strikes at me, or my interests, I will strike back with equal, preferably double, fury to teach him (them) a lesson. Forgiveness and attempts at reconciliation are just liberal religious sentimentality.

I must succeed in life by making myself more attractive to the people who count. This involves expressing only "approved philosophies" of the "in group" and pleasing those with the power to reward me.

To Remember

O Lord, who died demonstrating the need to reject the temptation to please the "in group," help me!

To Record

To Listen

God judges our world.
This judgment falls upon those
who live totally for themselves.
They are indifferent to the needs
of their fellowmen.
No matter how impressive their rituals
and religious exercises,
their lives are not pleasing to God.
              —Psalm 50 (Modern translation)

To Ponder

Throughout history power has been abused by selfish leaders who are really indifferent to the needs of their fellowmen. Politicians and prelates, dictators, executives in business, government, religion, education, and every area of society have fallen victim to this malaise. And so-called ordinary people, without real power, have shared in it by doing no better.

And yet, as the Psalmist goes on to say:

"God is at work in our world. He works in and through the lives of His children who are loyal and obedient to Him.... It is thus that He touches the lives of needy men...by way of the self-sacrificing love of His servants."

To Remember

O God, make me truly your servant by giving me the divine gift of self-sacrificing love.

To Record

To Listen

*God's creatures bear the consequences
of their self-centeredness,
and this world is distorted by their depravity.
But the Lord forgives those who turn to him
and makes them his childen and his servants
and through them seeks to heal
this world's gaping wounds.*

—Psalm 99 (Modern translation)

To Ponder

All of the distortions of this world—and of my own life—may ultimately be traced to self-centeredness and the over-compensations of false, insecure, and distorted ego.

But Divine forgiveness and the healing—or re-balancing—of those egos is the remedy.

This remedy must come from God through me and express itself in visible actions. Thus, I must learn to forgive those who have done me wrong, and teach others to do so. I must let the Divine love flow through me in un-selfish acts, in the healing of memories, of minds, and of bodies through the compassion that comes from learning to dwell in the Divine Presence.

To Remember

Give me, O Lord, the gift of your divine presence. . .that I may join you in healing the world.

To Record

To Listen

How great is my God!
He soars above our poor intellects
like a snow-capped mountain
over a sun-baked desert.
He scatters the profound theories of wise men
like leaves pushed around by a winter wind.
                    —Psalm 48 (Modern translation)

To Ponder

Here the Psalmist reminds us that we must not depend upon false gods—our own intellects, the theories of wise men, or the prosperity and might of our nations—to save us.

In the end, when all of these have failed, it is God himself who "shatters the assembled might of world governments as an earthquake levels a city" and who "reaches down in tenderness to earth's poor creatures and draws them to Himself."

In all of our interdependence and relationships on this planet it is so. It is only the Divine Reality and Presence which is ultimately trustworthy, reliable, and lasting.

To Remember

Let us cultivate the divine reality and presence in all of our relationships and interdependencies in this world.

To Record

July 30

To Listen

And faithful souls have yearned to see
On earth that kingdom's day.
The day in whose clear shining light
All wrong shall stand revealed,
When justice shall be throned in might,
And every hurt be healed.

—F. L. Hosmer

To Ponder

This is the eschatological hope of the Christian religion. Do you find it hard to believe, after reading your daily newspapers and watching the TV news of the world? Does your knowledge of history, and of human nature make this a liberal pipe-dream or visionary fantasy for you?

If anyone answers yes to these questions then he or she simply does not know God, His ineffable Power to work His will and ultimately to change the hearts of men...from beast-like to god-like character and behaviour.

To Remember

All of our relationships and interdependencies in this world must be based upon the sure knowledge of the reality of God's kingdom. He has given us a divine commandment to pray and work for its descent.

To Record

To Listen

So, because you are lukewarm, and neither cold nor hot, I will spew you out of my mouth.

—Revelation 3:15

To Ponder

"The moment one definitely commits oneself, then providence moves too.

All sorts of wonderful things occur to help one, that would never otherwise have occurred. A whole stream of events issues from the decision, raising in one's favor all manner of unforeseen incidents and meetings and material assistance which no man could have dreamed would come his way.

Whatever you can do or dream, you can begin it. Boldness has genius, power, and magic in it. Begin it now." (Goethe)

To Remember

I will commit myself this moment to the highest purposes of God and the universe, knowing that all the forces of Heaven and Earth will aid me.

To Record

UNIVERSAL TRUTHS

Even to speak of "universal truths" requires the recognition and acceptance of two assumptions. First, we must recognize that teachings exist which are known, valid and practical for everyone in the universe, and second, we must accept that these teachings are true and have been true for all time. These truths/teachings must therefore be valuable and have relevance for all peoples everywhere. Some would even call them spiritual or divine principles.

Indeed, these truths have come down to us through the passage of time and through many different races and schools of thought. Some believe these teachings to have come from the lost continent of Atlantis. Others believe they go back to the beginnings of the human race. These truths, it appears, have been known to advanced minds of all great civilizations of the past, even those lost many thousands of years ago. These truths need not establish the authority of their source because they express both the highest reason and intuition of human existence. They have always been available for those ready to receive them.

Interestingly, very little has been written about these truths. It is as if the innermost, secret and hidden part of the teachings passed directly from the mouth of the teacher to the ear of the pupil. The reason behind this secrecy (and elitism) is the potency of the message which may actually be dangerous if it falls into hands unprepared to deal wisely with such power. The principles, laws and truths, however, have been offered more freely to all who felt attracted to them, and no doubt special persons may be found around the world today—unknown and silent workers, who have mastered these truths on an inner plane.

Surprising as it may seem, these universal truths (laws) provide us with freedom, not bondage. This freedom, however, calls forth responsibility for it connects us with our true roots in the creative force or universal source of all life. Thus, we are called to be the captains of our souls, the masters of our fate.

In order for universal truths to manifest in our lives, we

must accept the necessity of change. Change brings movement, and all of nature, all of the cosmos, and all of us are eternally changing. Change, in fact, is a universal truth. Production brings change; growth (unfoldment) involves change, and dissolution is actually transformation. It has been said that change is the essential reality of this universe and that nothing within it is actually permanent.

It has also been said that the greatest of all the universal truths is based on this teaching: "We reap what we plant." Each of us has probably seen this thought in action in our own lives. In truth all religions carry at least an equivalent teaching within their doctrine.

Jesus himself left us these words:

> As ye would that others should do to you,
> do ye also to them likewise.
> Matthew 7:12

ABOUT THE AUTHOR

James E. Bonacci is a Divine Science minister who was a co-founder and served on the staff of the Community Church by the Bay in Newport Beach, California. He is a vocal musician, a counselor, and a free-lance writer. He also speaks and conducts workshops in Spiritual Psychology throughout the country. He resides in Santa Ana, California.

—the Editor

August 1

To Listen

The troubled mind is a troublemaker.
　　　　　　　　　—Edna St. Vincent Millay

To Ponder

God-Energy flows in the form of Creative Ideas. A clear mind is a clear channel for these Creative Ideas; a troubled or dark mind is a chaotic mess of misperceptions and ignorant conditioning. How do we clear our minds of those conditions that keep us from being a clear channel of God's Eternal Truth?

To become enlightened means to become full of light. As we clear our minds and let the light of God come into our lives it sheds wisdom and love on all aspects.

The way to enlightenment is through prayer and meditation. We cannot travel two roads at the same time. The more we pray and meditate on the principles of God, the less we will give energy to ignorant conditions (fear, hate, guilt, etc.). "Thou dost keep him in perfect peace, whose mind is stayed on thee, because he trusts in thee." (Isaiah 26:3)

To Remember

My mind is open to God's wisdom and guidance.

To Record

To Listen

In him we live and move and have our being.
—Acts 17:28

To Ponder

The very first eternal truth we must understand is that we are ONE with God. In Him we DO live and move, and there is no way to really separate ourselves from Him—except by our own ignorance and misperception (and that is only temporary). Separation is only an illusion, a false-image of self. More often, it is simple miseducation.

Anyone who thinks he is independent from God in any way is mistaken and, no doubt, reaping a miserable harvest. When we experience ourselves as part of a wholistic creation, we can more clearly realize our oneness with God.

To Remember

When an astronaut looks at the earth from outer space he sees only a unisphere.

To Record

August 3

To Listen

Who is the man that fears the Lord? Him will he instruct in the way that he should choose.

—Psalm 25:12

To Ponder

It is sometimes too easy to get all wrapped up in the material world. The urbanized, industrial-technological world of man is a plastic representation of reality. When we participate in it, without knowing full well that it is the kingdom of man, we run the risk of losing contact with our true Source.

The further we move away from nature—which is the pure material manifestation of God—the more difficult it is to maintain conscious union with our spiritual reality. Pray and meditate daily so as not to lose this contact, and HE will instruct us in the way we should choose.

The eternal truth of your being is that you are a physical manifestation of spiritual reality. Remind yourself every day.

To Remember

I release the desire to be independent and let my GOD-IDENTITY come forth.

To Record

To Listen

Love the Lord thy God with thy whole heart and soul and love thy neighbor as thyself.

—Matthew 5:48

To Ponder

Spiritual Love is eternal love. Love is the most important experience of our lives and, yet, it is probably the most misunderstood.

We are told that we can "make" love or "give" love. We think romantic love with all its complicated side effects is true love. This is because we are taught to equate love and sex as if they were the same thing. Sex is a *function*; love is an *essence*; it is our essential beingness. Love can be expressed through sex but sometimes is not. What we don't realize is that pleasure and pain are two ends of the same spectrum.

The alternative to pleasure and pain is happiness which is the result of spiritual joy. "But seek first his kingdom and his righteousness, and all these things shall be yours as well." (Matthew 6:33)

To Remember

I love my body as I love God's beauty expressed through all nature.

To Record

August 5

To Listen

And God saw everything that he had made, and behold, it was very good.

—Genesis 1:31

To Ponder

That which is good is that which lasts. This is the way we measure and discover eternal truth. Physical life, as beautiful or miserable as it can be, is temporary. It is not an eternal truth. Consciousness, however, is permanent and is an eternal truth.

Pierre Tielhard de Chardin and Emmet Fox are two great minds that have told us—*all life is consciousness.* Consciousness here is meant as spiritual awareness not the "conscious" dimension of the human reasoning mind. Spiritual awareness is the awareness of our participation with God, the good and all the aspects of God such as Love, Truth, Peace, Faith, Beauty, Gratitude, and Peace.

To Remember

To the extent that I practice love—to that extent I practice the presence of God.

To Record

To Listen

Earth's crammed with heaven, and every common bush afire with God.
                    —Elizabeth Barrett Browning

To Ponder

Nature in all its beauty and splendor is the physical manifestation of pure spirit. No wonder we are inspired and renewed when we visit or live within it.

Surely, God is in the city but so much harder to find beyond the many distractions of man-made objects. Whereas in nature, heaven jumps out at you in color, balance and grandeur—"And only he who sees takes off his shoes the rest sit 'round it and pluck blackberries."

Thank God for the inspired teachers all around us nudging us to open our hearts and let God out.

To Remember

Let me open my eyes that I might open my heart.

To Record

August 7

To Listen

I seem to have been only a boy playing on the seashore, and diverting myself in now and then finding a smoother pebble...whilst the great ocean of truth lay all undiscovered before me.

—Isaac Newton

To Ponder

Here we are struggling with the everyday experience of life, and someone comes along and says, "That's not the real thing; the real thing is beyond that."

Somehow, it doesn't seem fair to ask one to study the metaphysical reality of life when they haven't mastered the physical aspect. Yet, as Newton points out—our attention is diverted by the little things while the ocean of truth lies undiscovered before us. "For now we see through a glass darkly; but then face to face." (I Cor. 13:12)

Ironically, what the great teachers have been trying to tell us is that when we understand our spiritual reality, our physical nature "works" better. Often, it is all too easy to miss the forest because of the trees.

To Remember

I enjoy my life more fully when I see through eyes with spiritual dimension.

To Record

To Listen
Beauty through my senses stole, I yielded myself to the perfect whole.

—Ralph Waldo Emerson

To Ponder
Beauty is one of the eternal truths; it is a spiritual quality which is expressed through nature and creativity as the balance of color, sound, form, movement and other sense awarenesses. Beauty inspires; it promotes spiritual enlightenment.

Take time to expose yourself to the classic beauty of nature, art, music, dance and so forth that promotes balance, harmony and well-being. Avoid the pollution of beauty—excessive noise, confusing rhythms and forms, anything that promotes chaos and a disturbance of balance.

Only you and I can make the decision for ourselves as to what we will expose our minds and senses to. Don't let the mass hypnosis of the ego-world lull you into the sleep of separation.

To Remember
Fads come and go. Classic beauty is that which stands the test of time.

To Record

August 9

To Listen

To get wisdom is better than gold.

—Proverbs 16:16

To Ponder

All life is God. Only that which is God really exists; the rest is just an illusion and temporary. When we undertand this then we can understand that all life is one; it is whole, and we are part of this oneness or wholeness.

Since God is true wisdom and love, we are true wisdom and love. This is the reality of our consciousness, our spiritual awareness. It is this awareness that we seek to understand and allow to express itself in our physical dimension of experience. This is our number one priority—"Lay not up for yourselves treasures upon earth...but lay up for yourselves treasures in heaven..." (Matthew 6:19, 20)

Often, we are taught to believe that wealth, career, and personal relationships are our number one priorities. We learn to strive for *quantity* rather than *quality*.

To Remember

I clear my mind of all effort to be anyone or anything and allow that which I am to come through.

To Record

To Listen

With all thy getting—get understanding.
                                        —Proverbs 4:7

To Ponder

When we understand *who and what we are and what our purpose* is we will know *how* to change that which needs to be changed in our lives. Often, we go about it from the wrong direction and only delay our path back to wholeness.

expect to understand ourselves. But, this is what we do. We study the physical history and anatomy of mankind in hope of understanding who and what we are—when this is not who we are.

Religious dogma and state were kept separate by our constitutional orginators and rightly so—but God was recognized as our source. "...the separate and equal station to which the Laws of Nature and of Nature's God entitle them..." "...endowed by their Creator with certain inalienable Rights, that among these are Life, Liberty and the pursuit of Happiness."

To Remember

We govern our lives by spiritual laws—in God we trust!

To Record

August 11

To Listen

We and God have business with each other; and in opening ourselves to his influence our deepest destiny is fulfilled.

—William James

To Ponder

In the world of appearances we are subject to mass hypnosis—fooled into believing that which is not really so.

The only way to "open ourselves to His influence" is to establish a *free* and *clear* mind. A mind controlled by mass hypnosis or confused and driven by physical addictions (to drugs, alcohol, caffeine, sex, sugar, etc.) cannot be free and clear.

Whether we are aware or unaware of suffering in our lives, we can be sure this suffering means we are living out of harmony with God. Take time to reestablish *freedom* and *clarity* of consciousness.

To Remember

I stand guard at the window of my mind.

To Record

To Listen

Enthusiasm for the universe, in knowing as well as in creating, also answers the question of doubt and meaning.

—Paul Tillich

To Ponder

Faith is based on knowing, and knowing is based on understanding. We cannot have faith without understanding that our reality is essentially *spiritual* and *eternal*.

As we practice the ancient art of fasting, we will understand more. Whenever we think of fasting we think of not eating. However, it is more important for us to fast from pleasure and pain seeking desires which only continue to confirm our ego and our ignorance of God.

"Whatsoever things are true, whatsoever things are honest,...pure,...lovely,...think on these things." (Philippians 4:8) As we do this, our faith builds; everything begins to come into proper perspective, and healing and wholeness become a reality in our lives.

To Remember

I clear my mind and let God fill it with all his glories.

To Record

August 13

To Listen

Yet lackest thou one thing; sell all that thou hast and distribute unto the poor, and thou shalt have treasure in heaven.

—Luke 18:22

To Ponder

Not everyone has to give up all that they have materially to find and know God in their lives. This was an example, a lesson about unhealthy attachments. To more clearly understand our spiritual reality we must look at our physical and emotional attachments and addictions.

All addictions whether to money, food, chemicals (drugs) or relationships are consuming and limit us from experiencing the qualities of God. Envy and jealousy are two examples; domination and perfectionism are others. The lifting of these "heavy" burdens brings en-lightenment to our physical existence and consciousness.

Take inventory of your physical and emotional attachments. Are they preventing you from realizing your spirituality? Work on them one at a time; release them, and free your physical energy to express love and wisdom.

To Remember

The wholeness that I am can never be divided.

To Record

To Listen

Science...tells us that nothing in nature, not even the tiniest particle, can disappear without a trace. Nature does not know extinction. All it knows is transformation.

—Wernher von Braun

To Ponder

Few people have been spared the void of losing a loved one, and very, very few are ever prepared for such an experience. Forming attachments is a strong human need. In one sense, it confirms our existence, provides us the opportunity to love intimately and provides a security against the great unknown.

How much easier it would be to adjust if we knew that, that life we once shared is still existing at some level or dimension in a state of transformation. And, we are still one with that life.

Now, it is our job (as it always was) to form the ultimate attachment to God, and let his loving wisdom guide us anew.

To Remember

True love is universal; this new concept moves me to new heights of expression.

To Record

August 15

To Listen

For it is in giving that we receive; it is in pardoning that we are pardoned.

— St Francis of Assisi

To Ponder

Oddly enough, we human beings are born in a dependent and self-centered condition, and unless we learn differently, we stay that way, never realizing that it is our loving parents' self-sacrifice that provides our needs.

There is a truth of life that seems paradoxical, yet St. Francis understood it as did Jesus and other great teachers. It is—whatever you want or need the most in your life, start giving it away! If you want love—start giving love (friendship, praise, finances, etc.).

The ego is our physical consciousness. It can sometimes exert a great deal of control over us, forgetting that it is not a creation of itself and by itself. It is up to us to blend this identity with our spiritual identity.

If we didn't have good teachers in our early development—now is the time to look for those teachers and those lessons that will help us re-educate ourselves and open our lives to God's spirit. We can do it!

To Remember

I give myself in service to eternal life.

To Record

To Listen

Not what goes into the mouth defiles a man, but what comes out of the mouth, this defiles a man.
—Matthew 15:11

To Ponder

In an age of "tell it like it is" we often mistake emotional ventilation for freedom. Everyone is out expressing him/her self as if it were the way to become healthy.

Jesus was teaching us a valuable lesson about the power of words. So did John, "In the beginning was the word..."

Examine your thoughts before you express them, and you will spend much less time "pulling your foot out of your mouth." Eventually, you will be retrained and won't need to examine your thoughts so frequently.

The more clearly you understand who you really are—the more your words will come out guided by loving wisdom.

To Remember

Be sure your mind is engaged before you put your mouth in gear.

To Record

To Listen

If you had an enemy, and knew his heartaches and his anxieties, you would be disarmed of your hostility and claim him as a brother.

—Longfellow

To Ponder

Sitting in judgment on another is as old as life itself. In judging others we obviously judge ourselves since life is one.

Those who are pious are invariably the worst offenders. They usually have come out of a rigid religious background. They are caught in the "right-wrong," "sin-virtue," "clean-dirty," duality. This is not mature.

We can work at moving away from judgment and punishment to forgiveness and understanding. As we move in this direction, we can afford to love more freely. Through our understanding and forgiveness we become a free soul.

To Remember

I live in the spirit of understanding, compassion, and cooperation.

To Record

To Listen

Have no opinions; have no suffering.
                                        —Marcus Aurelius

To Ponder

It would be most advantageous for us to fast (abstain) from many mental conditions, especially those conditions that bind us to the world of error.

We become bound by our opinions (judgments) and lost to eternal truth which requires a free and open or clear mind to reveal itself.

Opinions only bind us to the world of duality. Love has no opinions; it stems from oneness.

Next time you find yourself forming opinions or passing judgments, gently remind yourself and discontinue. Affirm a statement of truth and apply it to yourself and the object of opinion.

To Remember

I am strong in the law of love.

To Record

To Listen

Ignorance is the only sin, and it is wholly forgivable.

—Jim Bonacci

To Ponder

The only sin is ignorance. It is the only reason we act contrary to our true nature which is oneness with God. Ignorance means "without knowing"—in other words, NOT KNOWING WHO AND WHAT WE REALLY ARE.

When we refer to the "ego" we are referring to the physical identity of man which sometimes gets lost in its own illusion of independent existence. Because of this it acts contrary to the interests of the whole by being selfish or self-aggrandizing. It operates in darkness or ignorance of God reality.

As more and more people become enlightened, more and more are drawn to the magnetic power of light, and darkness disappears. "Let your light so shine before men, that they may see your good works and give glory to your Father who is in heaven." (Matthew 5:16)

To Remember

God's light guides me toward freedom from ignorance/darkness.

To Record

To Listen

Our concept of God must be extended as the dimensions of our world are extended.
> —Pierre Teilhard de Chardin

To Ponder

The problem with ignorance is that it causes us to be limited by our beliefs. One can believe anything, but it might not be harmonious with reality or eternal truth. For example, one can *believe* that 1 and 9 equal 12, but that does not make it so. On the other hand, one might *disbelieve* that 1 and 9 equal 10, but that does not make him right. This is exactly how evil exists. It is an erroneous belief in a power which does not really exist.

To believe or disbelieve are two sides of the same spectrum. Each one fixates our awareness and limits our ability to be open, not to mention the fact that we might be wrong which complicates it even further.

The alternative to belief and disbelief is to *know*. "And ye shall know the truth and the truth shall make you free." (John 8:32) A belief is never certain; knowing is.

To Remember

I open and free my mind to experience more and more of God.

To Record

To Listen

And that day ye shall know that I am in my Father, and ye in me, and I in you.

—John 14:20

To Ponder

We must learn to be patient with ourselves and others as we seek to understand and realize our true being.

That which we have mislearned tends to hold fast and resists giving up its dominance in our lives. As a result, we see glimpses of truth, and, then, it seems to elude us as we slip back into our old patterns of conditioning.

We have all experienced some mistreatment and miseducation in our formative years which *we perpetuate* in our lives today. Let's all be patient and help each other unfold like a lotus flower or a rose.

To Remember

There is no clock in the realm of spirit; there is no time in our eternal being.

To Record

To Listen

This is the day which the Lord hath made; we will rejoice and be glad in it.

—Psalm 118:24

To Ponder

What truth is this passage telling us? It is telling us that being "fixed" on past experiences or future anticipations is one of the major problems of humankind. This produces anxiety.

Trying to change the past or worrying about the future is a way of trying to control life and a way of avoiding the responsibility of the present, in other words an escape.

Anxiety is just energy spinning its wheels, going nowhere. We cannot control our past or future. First of all, they don't even exist except in your mind. All we can control is what we will entertain in our minds today, right now. Since we cannot keep our minds on two things at the same time, it is to our advantage to keep our minds filled with the qualities of God. Keep teaching yourself about love and joy.

Remember, God is not in the past or future but only in the eternal now.

To Remember

I clear my mind of all barriers to God's light.

To Record

August 23

To Listen

I have not found Him. I am prepared to sacrifice the things dearest to me in pursuit of this quest.
—Mohandas K. Gandhi

To Ponder

God is elusive to the busy-busy human mind which is always struggling with the "needs and desires" of the human body and manipulated by profit oriented advertisers. One need only watch television advertising for one day to see what advertisers are attempting to hypnotize Americans to do or be. Fortunately, we are in control of whether we will be hypnotized or not.

We never really find *all* of God. But, every time we make a "spiritual connection" with some form of life we come to know God a little more. We make a "spiritual connection" when we *let* love guide our motives and activities.

To Remember

If I could see inside my enemy's heart I would see my own cares and concerns.

To Record

To Listen

God is inexpressible.... Nothing is comparable to him.... He is not at all what you have conceived him to be.

—St. Augustine

To Ponder

When St. Augustine says nothing is comparable to him he means no-thing. There is nothing that we can compare to God. God is Allness and it is not possible to imagine him, for when we do we limit him.

Jules Renard said, "God does not believe in our God." We manipulate our concept of God according to our beliefs or prejudices.

We would be far better off to stop believing in God and start knowing that God is at the heart of all reality and is a continual source of giving—love, joy, intelligence, truth, etc. Whether we are open to or aware of these gifts, and what we do with them, determines the quality of our life.

To Remember

I release all prejudices [prejudgments] and let God's gifts flow freely through me.

To Record

To Listen

For God, to me, it seems is a verb, not a noun.
—Buckminster Fuller

To Ponder

Buckminster Fuller was trying to show us that God is best described as active (verb) rather than static (noun). God CREATES; God LOVES; God GIVES and FORGIVES.

This will help us to understand that we actualize God in our lives by actualizing the qualities of God—i.e., creating, loving, giving and for-giving. To *believe* in God is a static non-actualized condition just as it is to *disbelieve* in God (atheism). "Thou believest that there is one God;...the devils also believe, and tremble." (James 2:19)

Religious people have believed in God for years and look at history. Obviously, mankind has yet to actualize God on a grand scale—"What doth it profit, my brethren, though a man say he hath faith, and have not works? Can faith save him?" (James 2:14) We are still on the Spiritual Frontier!

To Remember

Now *is* the time to *activate* God in my life. Yesterday is gone; tomorrow is but a vision.

To Record

To Listen

For unto every one that hath shall be given and he shall have abundance; but from him that hath not shall be taken away even that which he hath.
—Matthew 25:29

To Ponder

Spiritually speaking, the "survival of the fittest" refers to those who learn to love—just as, "to him that hath shall be given" implies. To him that hath the love of God in his heart—to him shall be given even more.

Those who have the love of God in their heart exude an air of beneficence. We feel better in their presence for they love us more than we love ourselves.

While if we are not clear in the love of God we are not able to keep what little we have.

It is a law of life, to know how to love is to know how to live in the true reality of our being—as one with God. The absence of love is the absence of God.

To Remember

To love is my true purpose and being. As I give up negative conditioning, love moves in to take its place.

To Record

To Listen

Judge not, and ye shall not be judged; condemn not, and ye shall not be condemned; forgive and ye shall be forgiven.

—Luke 6:37

To Ponder

One of the best ways to clear the mind of barriers is to stop *all* judgment! Every time we judge, no matter how great or small, we set up a barrier to our freedom. Imagine that! No, realize it! And, better yet, stop it!

Abstain from judgment—be quick to forgive. "Be ye therefore merciful, as your Father also is merciful." To be merciful is to be compassionate which means a "sympathetic consciousness of others' distress."

Since God is compassionate, then compassion is part of our true nature, and compassion is the result of understanding. Paul advised us, "Be not overcome of evil, but overcome evil with good." (Romans 12:21) "Owe no man anything, but to love one another; for he that loveth hath fulfilled the law." (Romans 13:8)

To Remember

I seek to love and understand, and leave judgment to God.

To Record

To Listen

The visible world is part of a more spiritual universe from which it draws its chief significance.

—William James

To Ponder

In his book, *Varieties of Religious Experience*, James drew the above conclusion and the following: "...union or harmonious relation with the higher universe is our true end." And, "...prayer or inner communion with the spirit of this 'higher universe'...is a process wherein...spiritual energy flows in and produces effects, psychological or material, within the phenomenal world."

One of the great things about eternal truth is when you hear it, really hear it, you know it is true because deep in your heart it is already there waiting to be uncovered. Our job is to be prepared to hear it by prayer and fasting from fear-provoking thoughts.

To Remember

Truth knocks at the door, and I open it.

To Record

August 29

To Listen

Our ultimate concerns are our faith.

—Paul Tillich

To Ponder

Perhaps the ultimate aim of life is to enjoy it, to move continually toward expressing the spiritual qualities of love, faith, joy and peace, and to be enthralled by the sheer mystery of life.

Faith means to live as a part of the whole of things in a unified cosmos. We can have faith that the world will work out its own destiny and so can use us, our mistakes as well as our creativeness.

Each of us, in our own day and in our own way, must come to our own conclusions about our own faith, our own life, our own destiny.

Faith does not need guarantees. It is there because of growing inner experiences. Faith maintains that one's innate potential is toward growth.

To Remember

The quality of my life is determined by the quality of my mental and physical activities.

To Record

To Listen

But love ye your enemies,... and ye shall be the children of the Highest; for he is kind unto the unthankful and to the evil."

—Luke 6:35

To Ponder

This is probably the most difficult lesson for anyone to learn. It is contrary to almost everything we see around us. We are still living by Moses' law of Exodus 21:24, "If any harm follow, then you shall give life for life, eye for eye, tooth for tooth etc." Which also says, "Whoever strikes his father or his mother shall be put to death." Exodus 21:15

would-be assassin and forgave him. I'm sure John Paul was greatly relieved by this act. In forgiveness we go free! "Let your light so shine before men, that they may see your good works, and glorify your Father which is in heaven." (Matthew 5:16)

To Remember

I fully and freely forgive my enemies and do what I can to help bring light to the world.

To Record

August 31

To Listen

The gloom of the world is but a shadow. Behind it, yet within reach, is joy.

—Fra Giovanni (1513 A.D.)

To Ponder

Joy is one of the hidden qualities of life. To find it we must be willing to look beyond what we see on the surface.

Wonder is one of the great emotions of mankind. It is not the same as "nosy curiosity" which is marred by hidden prejudices; it is an innocent, open mind searching and longing to discover meaning in the great mysteries of life.

Fra Giovanni goes on to say, "Life is so generous a giver, but we, judging its gifts by their covering, cast them away as ugly, or heavy, or hard."

Let wonder guide you to the hidden joys of life that are rich in spiritual abundance.

To Remember

What will happen to my life if I step out in faith today?

To Record

INNER PEACE AND OUTER STRENGTH

Inner peace is a universal need, but when we wonder how to achieve it, we are actually forgetting that we have only to tap into something which has always been available for us. Inner peace is! All we must do is open ourselves to it! It is the key to harmony in our lives and in the world. The person who has achieved inner peace is one who knows serenity of spirit and tranquility of mind.

When a connection is made with the inner storehouse of peace, buried deep within our being, an unlimited supply of strength is available to us. In the deep stillness, we come and touch and are touched by the spirit of peace which always assures us of a calmness of mind, gentleness of heart and humility of spirit.

In correspondence with Barbara Bunce, the author of the daily readings for this month of September, I have received some words on the subject of inner peace. I now share these thoughts with you.

"There are many ways of achieving the stillness and openness to God which we practice in meditation and contemplation. To focus on some potent thought received from another is part of the technique. In selecting the words to inspire us, we draw to ourselves inexhaustible resources of support and strength, both from the originator of the words and from the countless souls who have found the words a blessing in their own lives.

"As we draw peace, love and strength to us, so we may radiate those qualities out to the world, both during the time of silence and then in our outer life of human contacts. This process of radiation is at all levels. It is as if we were radio-active, not with the harmful energies normally associated with that term, but with the healing and peace-bringing energies which come from God.

"To grow in sensitivity to another's need; to be able to give the response which brings harmony where discord and hurt are met; to have strength to love and serve where there is no apparent reward; these are results of inner peace, and they create peace in countless small ways, the ripples spreading outwards beyond our immediate perception.

"Further, to offer our silence and inner peace to the world means that we are being used as generators of power for good beyond our knowing, and we are co-operating with the Angels of God in bringing about that final and universal peace which is the ultimate purpose of all being.

"Sometimes we can be uplifted into that sublime concept; sometimes we need to be met in our human littleness and need. May my selection of words of beauty, power and compassion be a source of further inspiration to my fellow pilgrims on the Way as they contribute their own offerings of prayer and service."

The responsibility and privilege for creating harmony and peace, which flow from our inner peace, rest upon us all. Our lives are strengthened outwardly by living in peace and harmony with each other. A fellowship or spiritual movement can be like a stream from which, in the long run, the reconciling spirit flows into all human relationships. As the stream begins to flow from the inward spring, we truly begin to *live*.

May we each find strength from the inner spirit of peace "...to guide our feet into the way of peace" (Luke 1:79) so that we can:

> *...agree with one another, live*
> *in peace and the God of love and*
> *peace will be with you.*
> II Corinthians 13:11

ABOUT THE AUTHOR

Barbara Bunce is Chairman of the Churches' Fellowship for Psychical and Spiritual Studies in Great Britain (a sister organization to SFF). A talented writer, healer, counselor, lecturer and workshop leader, Barbara is modest and humble concerning her considerable gifts. Having lived in India and Burma, Barbara currently resides in Exeter, England.

—the Editor

To Listen

To give light to those who live in darkness and the shadow of death, and to guide our feet in the way of peace.

—Luke 1:79

To Ponder

The need is as great now as ever it was when Zechariah, filled with the Holy Spirit and using the ancient words of Isaiah, uttered this prophecy about Jesus, soon to be born, and for whom his own new-born son, John, was to be forerunner and prophet.

When we, in our turn, use these words, we attune ourselves to ancient wisdom and continue the inspiration through the coming of Jesus the Christ and the Holy Spirit into our world and lives.

So in world needs in darkness and strife, and in individual needs in anxiety, fear or grief, we may invoke the Spirit of the Lord to bless our meditation for universal or individual healing and peace.

To Remember

Shine in our darkness, Lord, and hold us in your peace.

To Record

September 2

To Listen
Come now, little man, take time off for God....
Rest for a while in him;
enter the secret room of your mind.
—St. Anselm

To Ponder
It seems that even in what we assume to have been a much less pressurized age it was necessary for St. Anselm, gently and humorously, to encourage his contemporary "little man" to "put aside your busy-ness for a while" and to seek God.

And at times, however much we may be worried about the demands of family, home, office or clients, we too need to be reminded to enter the secret room of the heart or mind and there to establish, or confirm and strengthen the practice of waiting upon God. Thus we find the peace of mind which in due course allows all that is necessary to be accomplished with the added bonus and blessing of the divine touch.

To Remember
Before I embark upon my busyness this day, I rest for a while in God.

To Record

To Listen

Give me my scallop shell of quiet . . . my staff of faith to walk upon, my scrip of joy, immortal diet.

—Sir Walter Raleigh

To Ponder

The scallop shell is the pilgrim badge, said to have originated in medieval times from the plentiful by-products of the fishing industry in Northern Spain when thousands of pilgrims used scallop shells as water scoops as they arrived at the shrine of St. James of the Field of Stars (Santiago de Compostela).

With these words, therefore, Walter Raleigh evokes thoughts of pilgrim effort, attainment and peace. He adds the staff of faith, to lean upon when we weaken, and then he reminds us of joy—"immortal diet"—required by and provided for the pilgrim soul.

To Remember

In the quiet of meditation, I affirm my pilgrim quest, in faith and in joy.

To Record

September 4

To Listen

He who prays searches not only in his own heart, but plunges deep into the heart of the whole world.

—Thomas Merton

To Ponder

Silent prayer may seem an individual state but God is in all creation, and in practicing our own prayerful openness to God we change not only ourselves (in what may seem to us an infinitely small way) but affect many, known and unknown, seen and unseen, who are touched by us at soul level.

There is nothing selfish, therefore, in the pursuit of perfection of the self, if it is offered to God. It is divine work—personal yet universal. It is our ticket of passage, justifying the space we occupy. Our growth is part of the eternal work of re-creation, redemption.

To Remember

A short time of silence is an offering to God, and a gift from God.

To Record

To Listen

No man is an island entire of itself.... Never send to know for whom the bell tolls; it tolls for thee.

—John Donne

To Ponder

Continuing with yesterday's theme, Donne's familiar passage, with its insight into the oneness of all humanity, and stressing that "any man's death diminishes me," yet leaves us with the realization that equally any man's salvation enhances all life.

What a tremendous responsibility is thus put upon us. When we miss our time of quiet and prayer, we are not just depriving ourselves but depriving our neighbor, depriving humanity of one small effort which might have tipped the balance in today's sum total of good and evil.

To Remember

Help me, Lord, to play my part in the great scheme of creation.

To Record

September 6

To Listen

A charge to keep I have...to serve the present age....Arm me with jealous care....Help me to watch and pray.

—John Wesley

To Ponder

These first lines of each of the verses of a John Wesley hymn sum up the theme of the hymn, responsibility for one's own soul and one's part in the world.

Sometimes we are overwhelmed at the potentially catastrophic scope of world difficulties. "What can one person do?" is so often the cry. Yet through all recorded time, sages, teachers and saints have been telling us: "Seek!—"Knock!"—"Learn!"—"Pray!".

And the wonder of it is that we can begin right in our own homes, alone, and yet wonderfully not alone. Each step is followed by another, given, step.

To Remember

Help me to watch and pray.

To Record

To Listen

*Give us wisdom to perceive Thee...intelligence
to understand Thee...a heart to meditate upon
Thee, and a life to proclaim Thee.*

—St. Benedict

To Ponder

St. Benedict was very wise, and the order in
which he put these lines is very interesting. The
response of faith to God is so often instinctive,
from some deep inner spring of wisdom which
we do not even know we possess. Then comes
the questioning of the intellect, and the need to
understand.

Then intellect must rest, and the heart opens
itself to God in wordless trust, resulting in a life
which is a little more in tune with the divine,
and ready to be given to others in overt or
private world service.

To Remember

I know, I learn, I trust, and I share.

To Record

To Listen

The agent of healing is the Holy Spirit. The human instrument brings that Spirit fully down to earth.

—Martin Israel

To Ponder

In the dynamic peace of silent worship, the Holy Spirit infuses my being with new life, strength, inspiration. I may not feel dramatic changes in the moments of meditation; however, the process has begun, and I will not be unchanged.

When I leave my inner room, I will have taken another small step into wholeness, into awareness for myself, or another.

God will speak or act in me or through me because I have welcomed his Holy Spirit into my being.

To Remember

I am learning to be an instrument of the Holy Spirit.

To Record

To Listen

Lord, make me an instrument of thy peace.
—St. Francis of Assisi

To Ponder

To be an instrument might seem to imply passivity in the hands of the user, but to be instruments of the peace of God will demand more of us than passivity.

First there must come the chosen surrender and willed submission, the acquired and disciplined skills of silence and acceptance. Then must come the going out, as instruments, strung, tuned and ready, to be used to give love, consolation, healing, peace.

None of this is easy. This prayer, well-known and much used, is, one might almost say, a dangerous commitment. It is a life-changing prayer. Are we ready?

To Remember

In faith and trust I offer myself wholly to God's purpose for this day.

To Record

To Listen

Thou wilt keep him in perfect peace whose mind is stayed on Thee.

—Isaiah 26:3

To Ponder

These are words to be repeated and allowed to soak into one's whole being—ancient words, potent with association and use.

How can the world have continued to miss the mark for so long when over thousands of years the teachers and prophets have been such channels of wisdom and inspiration? Perhaps we attach too much importance to what in the world's history is such a short span of time.

But we are here now. This is our time. We have our part to play in the evolution of humanity. We still need continually to re-learn how to bring peace into our own lives and thus into the whole world. Still we must learn to "stay" our minds on the Eternal One who is Peace.

To Remember

I stay my mind on God—his peace flows into and through me.

To Record

To Listen

*Pray inwardly, even though you find no joy in it.
For it does good, though you feel nothing, see
nothing.*

—Mother Julian of Norwich

To Ponder

This fourteenth century mystic, com-
memorated in 1980 as a saint in the Church of
England, speaks to our troubled times from the
equally turbulent and suffering age in which
she lived. She spent her days in solitary devotion, yet with the window of her cell open to all
who might wish to consult her.

Her "Revelations of Divine Love" were
written in English, a first for a woman in that
time. All her teachings are based on a loving
God, despite the evidence of dreadful suffering
all around her. How much her faith is needed
today as more and more we become aware of
and share helplessly in global suffering.

To Remember

*Though I cannot always or often see results, I
keep faith in silent offering.*

To Record

September 12

To Listen

You, dear Lord, show us completed man, man as God always meant him to be, man as he can become by your grace.

—Bishop George Appleton

To Ponder

Sometimes it is hard to achieve the tranquillity of contemplation; then it is good to meditate, to dwell on a scene in the life of our Lord. There is much to choose from—Jesus as a child, teacher, compassionate friend, prophet, healer, Son of Man, Son of God, dying but still in command, triumphantly raised, victor over death and evil, perfect Love.

Choose just one scene; dwell on it; enter into it. "I am with you always, yes, to the end of time." Yes, in and out of time, He is there, and He is here.

To Remember

Dear Lord, by your grace, help me to follow in the way.

To Record

To Listen

God be in my head, and in my understanding.
God be in my heart, and in my thinking.
                                    —Old Sarum Psalter

To Ponder

This so well-loved medieval hymn seems to transpose sense as we would accept it today. Surely "understanding" comes from the heart and not the head? And "thinking" comes from the head and not the heart? Nevertheless, that is how we are given the words, and we are therefore given far more upon which to ponder.

Today's lines might well inspire us to realize that the love of God in our heads and hearts will affect all our judgments, comments and responses to those we may meet, so that however much they may "deserve" our sharp or harsh reaction, we know that it won't do. We have asked for the insight of love.

To Remember

Lord, fill my head and heart with love this day.

To Record

September 14

To Listen

I count on not being idle in Heaven, for it is my wish to continue to work for the Church and for souls.

—St. Thérèse of Lisieux

To Ponder

Solitary prayer is never really solitary. The great company of heaven, the ministry of angels, the communion of saints, however one likes to think of it, is ever active.

We strike a note with our uplifted hearts or thoughts, and as we are still, we become one with the universe of love. The greatness and complexity of it is beyond our imagining, but we can be sure that our time of silence is integrated into the great scheme in such a way that we have contributed, just as we have received. The unseen servants of God weave our prayers into the whole fabric of the world's salvation.

To Remember

I offer my time of silence in world service.

To Record

To Listen

The universe has been conquered when you have won. Your own Christ has conquered sin and death.

—John M. Watkins

To Ponder

Each day we begin the work afresh, and each time we come into our own silence we are working, not just for ourselves but for all humanity. But it has to begin here, right in our own home, right in our own hearts. Whatever system of relaxation, meditation or self-discipline we may follow, it is only necessary to offer it to God in the name of Jesus the Christ for our work to become part of the Christ consciousness, the kingdom of heaven within which is ever working to bring all creation into the light.

To Remember

I open my heart to Christ, and the Christ child within me grows stronger.

To Record

September 16

To Listen

Let nothing disturb you; let nothing frighten you; all things pass; God never changes.

—St. Teresa of Avila

To Ponder

When we are disturbed or frightened, it might not seem much comfort to be told that all things pass, or even that God never changes! Yet in our times of need, we know how much we can draw from the proven strength of another.

The words above, so often quoted, ring absolutely true because through them we know that the personality and greatness of soul of one who has triumphed speak to us. St. Teresa, with courage, strength, humor and shining faith overcame all the obstacles of life in sixteenth century Spain, to become a leader and inspirer of countless men and women in the centuries to follow. She *knew* and loved God. We may trust her.

To Remember

I speak the words of St. Teresa and draw on her faith and strength.

To Record

To Listen

Lord God, you have made us for yourself, and our hearts are restless until they find their rest in you.

—St. Augustine of Hippo

To Ponder

Why God made us the way He did is hard to understand. Although countless explanations, religious, philosophical, mystical and scientific have been given through history, deep in our human hearts honestly we must confess that if we had made the world we would have done it differently! We cannot understand the necessity for the suffering of little children, for deliberate and vicious cruelty, for broken hearts and mental self-torture, and for apparently natural disasters. But we know, too, that deeper still within us is the spark that glows at the thought of God; the voice that cries out in our extremity to God; and the soul that finally acknowledges that St. Augustine spoke truly.

To Remember

In the silence I rest in the assurance of my oneness with God.

To Record

September 18

To Listen
Drop Thy still dews of quietness till all our strivings cease.

—Francis Whittier

To Ponder
In this fourth verse of his hymn "Dear Lord and Father of mankind" the Quaker writer conveys the very essence of peace.

Dew on the grass is associated with quietness in nature, so a picture of tranquillity is at once established. Then, although we know that we have to be active, accept responsibility for our own lives, and, yes, strive, yet so often we aim so busily for the wrong target that we miss the opportunity for something more worthwhile. So we must learn to let go the strain and stress of self-dominated lives, and to become aware of a greater order and an inward peace.

To Remember
Thy still dews of quietness imbue me with Thy peace.

To Record

To Listen

Be still and know that I am God.

—Psalm 46:10

To Ponder

In eight words is enshrined a call which can take a lifetime to follow. We can train ourselves in stillness, and can experience or practice the presence of God; then something comes, steals over us, or arises in our inner depths which we recognize as being an intimation of the touch of God. Is this knowing? Or we can read and study, and acquire intellectual concepts. Is this, too, part of knowing? Then we can dwell on "I Am" as the great name for God—"Before Abraham was, I am"—the mighty words of Jesus; and filled with awe we realize that human limitations bring us only to the footstool of the Almighty.

Yet He has said: "Be still—and know."

To Remember

In the stillness God gives what we are ready to receive and know of him.

To Record

September 20

To Listen

We may make an oratory of the heart wherein to retire from time to time to converse with God.
—Brother Lawrence

To Ponder

"Practicing the presence of God at the kitchen sink" is the accepted picture of this seventeenth century mystic. However, it was not in a comfortable, modern kitchen that he achieved his mastery but in the bustle of a vast monastic kitchen, cooking for the whole community, with regular periods spent in the chapel.

Brother Lawrence was lame, and did not like cooking which he came to after a stormy life as a soldier, and he had to work through much anxiety and remorse. Yet his innate holiness and goodness shone through so that even in his own lifetime Parisians of all ranks sought him out. Now he is an inspiration to the twentieth century.

To Remember

In this time of quiet, let me establish an oratory of the heart for today.

To Record

To Listen

Never give a hollow greeting of peace, or turn
away when someone needs your love.

—Rule of St. Benedict

To Ponder

To be real is all that matters. To live in readi-
ness to meet our neighbor's need (however
weary we may be, however difficult that other
person may seem to be) takes more than good-
will. It demands denial of self, it requires the
ability to put self on one side so that our love
may in fact be God's love, for which we are
prepared channels. The daily practice of silent
prayer and openness to God helps that preparation, so that when occasion arises it can truly
be "not I, but Christ in me."

To Remember

Lord, help me to be ready to give whatever is
needed this day.

To Record

September 22

To Listen

We need silence to be able to touch souls. The energy of God will be ours to do all things well.
— Mother Teresa of Calcutta

To Ponder

The time spent alone is a vital source of strength and sensitivity. To be sensitive to others requires the strength not to be wearied or overcome by the pain in the world. Yet even that strength is not truly ours, but is given more and more as we train in the service of the Lord.

So, open and aware, sensing the need of others, we tread gently around their pain, and are their strength when they have none, and their comfort when they see only darkness.

To Remember

May my soul be strengthened and filled with love to spare.

To Record

To Listen

Do not let your hearts be troubled; trust in God still, and trust in me.

—John 14:1

To Ponder

Jesus speaks these words still; they linger in the air; we may attune ourselves and receive them at any time. Their resonance is eternal.

It is not easy to imagine the horror and pain already foreshadowed when the words were spoken. Jesus knew what was to happen. He wanted to prepare His disciples, and strengthen them at the same time. All around were menacing forces, oppression, darkness, death. Impending loss of the beloved Master cast its shadow over them all. But they must trust in the purposes of Divine Love.

To Remember

However great the forces of evil, may my heart ever trust in thee, Lord.

To Record

September 24

To Listen

O Joy! O wonder and delight! O sacred mystery!
My soul a Spirit infinite! An image of Deity!

—Thomas Traherne

To Ponder

Sometimes the world sparkles with beauty, of nature, or of human love and nobility. All creation seems to shout of the grandeur of God's purpose. A scene of beauty takes the heart; a deed of courage inspires the imagination; simple goodness moves one near to tears. And it is indeed a joyous thought that this is the hidden theme to which we all contribute. Beauty, truth and goodness are images of God. All else is passing and cannot survive.

Then it is indeed wonderful to reflect that God has made us in His image. We are part of the wonder and beauty. It is natural for us to be channels of His love.

To Remember

Praise the Lord, O my soul, and all that is within me praise his holy name.

To Record

To Listen

Out of his infinite glory may He give you the power through His spirit for your hidden self to grow strong.

—Ephesians 3:16

To Ponder

When we seek God in the silence we are never depending on our own strength or resources. Alone, we might manage for a while, but soon the well would run dry. As it is, we are, as St. Paul says, asking Christ to live in our hearts. His love, which is limitless, opens us to the fullness of God, Whose power can do infinitely more than we can ask or imagine.

In his own life, St. Paul demonstrated over and over the depth and grandeur of that power working in and through a dedicated follower of Jesus Christ. Still today the need is there, and the power is there, to nurture and strengthen our inmost selves.

To Remember

In the silence I offer my inner life to be strengthened and glorified in Christ.

To Record

September 26

To Listen

In that light which shows thee all this, stand; go neither to the right nor to the left.

—George Fox

To Ponder

We are being told not to rely on our own judgment and thoughts, but to dwell in the light which will show us all we need to know. As St. Augustine has said, it is the function of perfection to make us know our imperfections; and, encouragingly, that when we know our imperfections we are progressing more than if we thought ourselves perfect.

There are so many teachers and masters; so many distractions and apparent setbacks; but always we can return, to centre ourselves once again on Christ, the perfect Light.

To Remember

Throughout the day I bring my thoughts back to the theme: "The Light of Christ."

To Record

To Listen

God has created me to do him some definite service. I am a link in the chain. I shall be an angel of peace.

—Cardinal Newman

To Ponder

In this meditation the Cardinal develops the theme that we may not know what God has intended us to do but He will still use us to do His work, providing we follow His commandments.

Developing this trust in God's unknown purposes and, often, unseen results, is part of the work of the life of faith. Being centered upon God and open to His direction (whatever the trials and distractions of the day) is the product of times of silent prayer and meditation.

Then what greater encouragement than to think that our short moments of peace are contributing vitally to the peace of the world.

To Remember

I am a vital link in the chain. Help me, Lord, to be faithful.

To Record

September 28

To Listen

Jesus the man spoke to us and through him the Christ Spirit touched our world for all time.

—Anon.

To Ponder

The mysteries of resonance and time come into this: time past and time to come, and always time present. The words of Jesus reverberate in our inmost being. We have only to hold them silently in our consciousness, and we are part of the timeless circumstances in which they belong; and something of world essence is imparted to us.

On the Mount of the Sermon, by the shores of Galilee, at the foot of the Cross, on the road to Emmaus, the words burn in our hearts and we achieve a little more of that love and peace which the Lord offers endlessly to all who seek so that they may in their turn be world servers.

To Remember

Lord, may your words warm my heart and help me to love.

To Record

To Listen

That these Thy precious gifts may radiate through me and overflow the chalice of my heart.
—Frances Nuttall

To Ponder

The Chalice Prayer speaks of the precious gifts of light and love, and the prayer is printed in such a way that it takes the shape of a chalice.

It is a beautiful concept. When any vessel is filled it overflows, and one can imagine this chalice of the heart being so filled with God's love that the shining glory flows out in all directions. Thus, private prayer becomes an act of service to the world, radiating joy, serenity and peace.

To Remember

Father, I raise the cup of my heart to thee to be filled to overflowing with thy love.

To Record

To Listen

*I am the Light of the world; anyone who follows
me will not walk in the dark; he will have the
light of life.*

—John 8:12

To Ponder

A tremendous statement and a tremendous
promise, acted upon through the centuries and
found to be valid. Yet only now, as quantum
physics increases our knowledge of the proper-
ties of light, do we begin to see that claim and
that promise unfold into even deeper valida-
tion.

So we see Jesus as the Light of the World in
all dimensions. Dwelling in Him we become
part of that Light, His people on earth, yet also
part of a great company of the Spirit, seen and
unseen.

Taking the Light as our inspiration and our
life we play a vital part in bringing peace, joy
and healing into all levels of being.

To Remember

*I dwell in the light of the Lord, part of his uni-
versal and eternal life.*

To Record

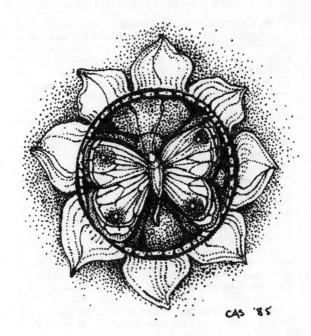

CAS '85

LOVE AND THE VIRTUES

One of the most widely used words, in all of the languages of the world, is the word *LOVE*. Each of us has spoken it at one time or another, and it can be felt yet longed for at the same moment within our hearts. It is understood, yet not understood by our minds. It calls forth to us from the very center of our being, and it seems to say: accept yourself; love yourself, and in being loved your giving of love comes naturally.

Love calls us to look at the person beside us, and at everyone we meet, and to see that the spiritual love which is the *core* of our being is likewise the *core* of their being. It encourages us to see not what they look like, or what they have or haven't done, to hear not what they say or do not say, but to sense who they truly *are*. They are divine spirits through whom the spirit of giving—that is, the spirit of love—can flow, and the greatest aspect of their giving, and our giving, is the ability to recognize and affirm the true *identity* in ourselves and in others.

Though we may act out the prodigal son or daughter scenario, we know that the love deep within our being is waiting to be expressed to those around us. This love tunes us into another and into the light in the crystal, the blade of grass, the bloom of the flower, the life of the animal, and everything else in the universe.

Love (Charity) has been known as one of the seven cardinal virtues (which go back to the time of St. Ambrose). Four of these virtues are referred to as natural, and three are referred to as theological. *Love*, regarded as love in Perfection—that is, high regard for our neighbor, is grouped with *Faith*—wholeheartedly believing and trusting and *Hope*—reliance on and expectation of the Good. These cardinal virtues hinge on the four chief virtues. Among these, *Justice* is that which has integrity and honesty, and is fair—creating a state of harmony. *Temperance* refers to a blending process which produces a sense of regulated and self-controlled moderation in action, thoughts and feelings. *Fortitude* refers to strength and firmness of mind expressed with courage and with the power of prolonged endurance. *Prudence* refers to wisdom shown through the exercise of reason, with foresight and discretion.

In some of the dialogues of Plato (with Socrates), the thought is expressed that if virtue were identical with knowledge, it could be taught and learned just as geometry is. If it were a habit, it could be acquired by practice. Virtue, however, is not come by through either practice or teaching. Instead, "virtue comes to the virtuous by the gift of God." (Plato).

The potential for being virtuous is the Gift of Love—the true nature of the soul's expression. The object of this love is love—love expressed unconditionally as goodness. Each of us can serve as a channel through which this love flows, and thus we will become beneficial presences in the world. This calls us to think on love and the other virtues, and it calls us to discipline our thoughts in order that they become loving thoughts. This love has the power to transform us into living expressions of our spiritual nature. May we this month recognize anew, as we think about the deeper meaning of virtue, the truth in the words:

> There is no fear in love, but
> perfect love casts out fear.
> I John 4:18a

ABOUT THE AUTHOR

James D. Ulness, a very understanding psychologist, is on the faculty at Concordia College. He serves on the Executive Committee and Council of SFF, speaks and conducts workshops at SFF retreats and chapter meetings, at psychology conferences and meetings, and in churches. He resides in Moorhead, Minnesota with his wife Pam and their two sons.

—the Editor

October 1

To Listen

Virtue is the most pleasing and valuable possession in the world.

—Plutarch

To Ponder

"Surely love is more valuable than virtue," you may ask. Love, however, is not a possession, and without virtue there can be no love. Love is the highest virtue. Though joy and wisdom are possessions, virtue is the prerequisite for both. Without virtue there can be no joy, and the highest virtue brings the highest joy. The history of humanity traces a spiral path of development on which growers progressively work on major qualities of soul as they pass through the "seasons" of the great cycle of life.

Esoteric history teaches that two "seasons" ago Beauty was the quality being developed, last "season" Truth, and this "season" Virtue, doing the Good. Since the *work* of these "seasons" is the will of God, we too may say, with the Master Jesus, "Surely I must be about my Father's business."

To Remember

Plato said, "All the gold on earth is not worth so much as virtue." Imagine, a "gold rush" on virtue?

To Record

To Listen

Without virtue, happiness cannot be.
—Thomas Jefferson

To Ponder

A life without happiness—you shudder at the thought of it. But, what is happiness? From where does it come? Happiness comes from functioning according to your design. We experience a good feeling when we exercise our muscles, use our minds, and our senses. Functioning physically or emotionally brings some happiness, but if you are not also functioning well mentally and spiritually, this happiness is short-lived. The spiritual student often neglects working at physical or mental activities, and then wonders why he or she isn't really happy. When we function as *whole* persons, according to our design as physical, emotional, mental, and spiritual creatures, there is a sense of well-being and a deep, abiding happiness. Any growth towards wholeness brings joy and happiness—the more complete the wholeness, the more complete the joy.

To Remember

Thomas Fuller was right when he said "If you can be well without health, you may be happy without virtue."

To Record

October 3

To Listen

To starve is a small matter, to lose one's virtue a great one.

—Kang-Hsi

To Ponder

How important is virtue? Even if you were starved sick, it would not be a sickness unto death, for "death" is not of the physical body. Death, real death, is failure to grow. With the loss of virtue, growth comes to an end.

The Christian Bible says there is one "unforgivable sin" and that is "the sin against the Holy Spirit." The Holy Spirit, as "the Lord and Giver of Life," calls each one to life, to growth.

As long as a person refuses or resists growth, life is hopeless. But then, like Lazarus, one can be roused to life if only one hears the call.

To Remember

When in the tomb of living death, be still and listen to your name being called, "Lazarus, come forth!"

To Record

To Listen

Virtue is beauty.

—William Shakespeare

To Ponder

We, at the present point in our development, have a certain freedom to give an impression or appearance on the outside which may differ significantly from what we are on the inside. For example, we can look and act friendly toward someone while feeling angry or hostile at them; give the appearance of being sad when someone else is hurting; or tell a lie with a straight face. We are great pretenders.

Esoteric teachings say that when a being truly reflects in outer appearances and behavior what is on the inside, this reflection produces a radiance of beauty which can be seen on certain planes clairvoyantly.

When we get our outer life to reflect what we truly are on the inside, when we act fully in accordance with our inner principles, we will be beautiful beyond measure.

To Remember

By the next great "season" we will not be able to say "Beauty is only skin deep."

To Record

October 5

To Listen
Virtue is harmony.

—Pythagoras

To Ponder

All persons are filled with conflicts that they strive to reduce. There are two ways they try to deal with this tension. The easy way, which does not lead to growth, is to deny, reject, or repress the aspects of themselves that are in conflict. This way, however, leads to a false sense of peace, for the inner conflict is only covered over and can emerge anytime like a threatening volcano. Much energy is expended day and night to prevent eruption. The other way to deal with inner conflicts is the way of synthesis. As healthy growers recognize and accept all of their conflicting aspects, they see that each has its opposite, like point and counterpoint, which together blend into something far better than each alone.

To Remember
"Virtue is the state of mind which tends to make the whole of life harmonious" Zeno
May we find it so.

To Record

To Listen

*Virtue is the middle ground between two vices,
the one of excess and the other of deficiency.*

—Aristotle

To Ponder

If we have behaviors that we particularly enjoy or are good at, we tend to go overboard and do them in excess. This tendency fits in with our social conditioning that "if something is good, more is even better." Likewise, our unconscious assumes, if something is bad, even less of it is better. This either/or thinking is standard Picean Age mentality. In many areas of our lives we need to move out of all-or-none thinking towards the notion of *optimal* amounts. How much of something is optimal? A good rule of thumb is the "golden mean" of the Greeks. There are some exceptions to this that we can learn, but by and large the best is the middle range between too much and none at all.

To Remember

Better to be found amongst the mean than in the standard deviations.

To Record

October 7

To Listen
Virtue is the fount whence honor springs.
                                        —Marlowe

To Ponder
St. Paul says in his letter to the Philippians, "whatever things are true, whatever things are noble, whatever things are just, whatever things are pure, whatever things are of good report, if there is any virtue and if there is anything praiseworthy—meditate on these things." Then Paul adds, "The things which you learned and received and heard and saw along these lines, these *do*, and the God of peace will be with you."

To Remember
"To do the honorable thing," in my heart I will let it ring.
                    —To the tune from *Man of La Mancha*

To Record

To Listen

Love your fellow men!
> —Confucius' definition of virtue

To Ponder

To love your fellowmen means to allow them to become what they were meant to be, to really care for them with "unconditional positive regard," as Carl Rogers would say. Genuine caring for others is to be sensitive to their growth needs. To see what love demands in the situations of life is *to hear* the call of the Spirit of Love saying "Follow Me." To respond to the call means *to do* the loving thing, which is virtue.

Love is that force which moves all things towards wholeness, harmony, and integration. This love, however, cannot be expressed as an isolated unit of consciousness. You can only know love in relationship with another. This relationship with one may lead to a relationship with many. And, when you come to know love as a relationship to the All, you know God.

To Remember

He who knows love, knows God.
> —John the Beloved

To Record

October 9

To Listen

Virtue is the only ground for friendship to be built upon.

—Thomas Fuller

To Ponder

Healthy growth involves an ever increasing consciousness of self, but individuation cannot be achieved without relatedness to another person. "The unrelated human being," Jung says, "lacks wholeness, for wholeness can be achieved through the soul, and the soul cannot exist without its other side, which is always found in a *You*." We all need at least one other to grow with through each phase of life, a "spiritual buddy." The best, the highest good, that you can do for the other is to help him or her become self-actualized. Real caring precludes any possessive attachment or desperate clinging to the other. As the circle of friendship widens, you acquire a whole set of spiritual kin who are your true brothers and sisters in the Spirit of Love.

To Remember

The bondes of vertue binde more straightly than the bondes of blood.

—Stefano Guazzo

To Record

To Listen

The chief good is the exercise of virtue in a perfect life.

—Aristotle

To Ponder

A perfect life is to be what one was created to be. Such a person would always act in accordance with the highest good. Although life, as we know it, is a process of becoming. Growers are ever striving for that perfect goal. The chief good is always and forever the exercise of virtue, to know the good, and then to do it.

One needn't question endlessly "What is the good?" If one strives to live up to the highest conception of goodness one can muster at that moment in one's development, that is virtue. With such striving, no matter how high or low this might be on an absolute scale of goodness, an interesting thing happens—a person's conception of goodness rises. And, in its rising, we are lifted up.

To Remember

Virtue is applying the best that one knows to the best of one's ability.

To Record

October 11

To Listen

If you adorn yourself with the highest virtue, the whole world will follow you.

—Ancient Chinese Proverb

To Ponder

At the very core of every human being is the knowledge of how the bits and pieces must come together to bring the whole world into being. This knowledge operates as a dynamic force, moving and impelling one toward that perfect world. If there were no resistance, all would fly immediately to their perfect place in the grand scheme of things, like so many iron filings around a magnet. But, human desires, distorted by selfishness and conscious ignorance of the whole, lead in other directions. The fact that unconscious inherent tendencies towards the perfect state are at cross-purposes with the conscious desires and are brought to the fore by the presence of a model of perfection, society is forced to eliminate the "perfect" ones who appear in history. They are put to death.

To Remember

All who lead are prepared to sacrifice.

To Record

To Listen

Virtues lose themselves in self-interest.
                                        —La Rochefoucauld

To Ponder

In the grand scheme of things, the Divine Plan which the Masters know and serve, the process of becoming for every order of being, can be summed up in one sentence. Evolution is the process of transition from taking to giving. In the beginning, a creature takes completely. This taking is necessary and good in the growth process. There could be no growth without it. Early in the process a little giving begins and this increases with maturation. Narcissism, being enamored with shallow love of self, is overcome as the Spirit of Love transforms one into an unconditional giver. Sacrifice becomes more and more an integral part of growth until one eventually becomes an All-Giver. Self-sacrifice is the paradox, that one must lose oneself in order to find oneself.

To Remember

Receiving is as important as giving in the process of growing.

To Record

October 13

To Listen
Long and steep is the path to virtue.

—Hesiod

To Ponder

Throughout childhood and youth the formative forces that shape one's life are heredity and environment. In humans the social environment is an especially powerful shaping force. The home, school, church, and community affect us far more than is generally believed. There comes a time, however, when responsibility for growth, development, and indeed, even for one's destiny, must fall more and more on an individual's own shoulders. This is an awesome and fearful task from which many shrink. Others, like Jonah, try to flee from their calling, but it hounds them relentlessly down the corridors of life until they finally must face it. Deep inside they know that Nature and the gods only develop a human being so far, and then it is up to each individual to take on the task of becoming what he or she was created to be—a spirit-being of freedom and love.

To Remember
He cannot be virtuous that is not rigorous.

—George Herbert

To Record

To Listen

Wisdom is knowing what to do next; virtue is doing it.

—David Starr Jordan

To Ponder

There are many times when we don't know what to do next and we wish we had more wisdom, but the real struggle these days is in applying what we already know. St. Paul expressed this well when he said, "The good that I would, I do not, and the evil that I would not, that I do." The greatest homage we can pay to truth, Emerson says, is to use it. The Christian Bible says "To him that knoweth to do good and doeth it not, to him it is sin. That is why Thomas Fuller remarked, "Virtue is praised by all, but practiced by few."

Virtue is not for the weak or the lazy. Ah!, But, we can be courageous. We can rise to the challenge. We can take heart in the fact that we have been given free will to act in this matter.

To Remember

There is nothing to it, but to do it!

To Record

October 15

To Listen

Through virtue lies the one and only road to peace.

—Juvenal

To Ponder

"Let there be peace on earth, the peace that was meant to be." Peace within, and peace without—what are the things that make for peace?

Making peace with self leads to peace in the world. There is a sequence in which this can occur. An old Chinese proverb says that righteousness in the heart leads to harmony in the home, and this in turn leads to order in the nation, and this, to peace on earth.

Righteousness in the heart starts out in children as a sense of fair play, becoming the sense of justice in the more mature adult, and, in those influenced by the Christ, it becomes love in action.

To Remember

Allow the spirit of love to touch your heart that you may work for peace.

To Record

To Listen

Folks who have no vices have very few virtues.
—Abraham Lincoln

To Ponder

Self-discovery is so important that we need to approach it in as many ways as possible. One way is to consider our strengths and our weaknesses. Sometimes it is difficult to list these out, but our greatest strengths and our most glaring faults are generally the easiest to note, and they are apt to give us very useful insights about ourselves. A peculiar thing we discover is that it is usually the overextension of our strengths which produces our faults, for example, persistence can become stubbornness. Likewise, if we examine closely our faults we are apt to find some strengths.

To Remember

Even the holy are not without faults. There is "hope for the flowers."

To Record

October 17

To Listen
The highest virtue is always against the law.
                              —Ralph Waldo Emerson

To Ponder
The noble is always beyond the norm. From the time we are born, however, we are praised for following and blamed for not following society's norms. Later, if we should start acting out of ideal principles, it will be perceived by many as being unlawful. Since we have spent most of our lives building allegiance to the representatives of our culture (parents, relatives, teachers, pastors, authority figures), and such a short time learning to stand up for our own inner principles, we may even have a sense of guilt for having violated the ways of our people. It takes great inner strength, courage, and self-confidence to go against tremendous social pressure to conform.

To Remember
Blessed are the nonconformers, for they shall see the ideal; but the fate of the "lemmings" is set.

To Record

To Listen

We need greater virtues to sustain good fortune than bad.

—La Rochefoucauld

To Ponder

Creative tension, inner opposing energies, is a tension that produces growth. When life is too easy, we tend to become complacent. The dynamic energy is gone, and we coast along with the status quo without growing at all. Ordinary growth stimuli may be dismissed or ignored so as not to disturb a rather nice, comfortable situation. Eventually, though, a perceived crisis, a hinderance, a hurdle, or a trial upsets our applecart. These difficulties may be the very challenges we need to stimulate growth. It isn't necessarily the gods who send these calamities. The higher unconscious may create them or draw us to them as deemed necessary for our higher good.

To Remember

In good times it is easy not to stretch; in bad times we must.

To Record

October 19

To Listen

Be noble! And the nobleness that lies in other people, slumbering, but never dead, will rise in majesty to meet thine own.

—J. R. Lowell

To Ponder

There is nothing better than to exemplify virtue, that is, living in all times and places, according to one's highest conception of the Good, the True, and the Beautiful. This will tend to bring out the best in them, ennoble them.

St. James said, "Faith without works is dead." The Master Jesus said, "By their fruits ye shall know them," and "A good tree does not bear bad fruit." Likewise, without virtue, nobleness in the soul is dead. When nobleness is alive in the soul, the person can only do that which is good in the long run.

To Remember

Virtue alone is the unerring sign of a noble soul.

—Nicolas Boileau

To Record

To Listen

Virtue glories not in the spoil, but in the victory.
—Dekker and Webster

To Ponder

In the early stages of development many spiritual growers focus too much on the possible benefits of acting virtuously. It is in the very process of victory over the temptation to act in less noble ways that one should find delight, rather than in the benefits that might be gained thereby. A frequent form of ego inflation is in thinking, "If I'm real good I'll win God, or the right to receive mystical/psychic experiences, etc."

To Remember

Victory over self means self-mastery.

To Record

October 21

To Listen

He who follows the path of virtue becomes as a little child.

—Lao Tze

To Ponder

True self-knowledge and true love lead to humility that is childlike—open and eager to learn, not puffed up with arrogance. Since the mature, adult, ego personality was developed to cope with reality, to have to give up this function of the ego, makes a person feel extremely vulnerable. This step, however, is asked of all spiritual growers. It, therefore takes strength and courage to become humble.

Now, to act virtuously never takes one on a pre-planned course. It takes flexibility to sacrifice the ego plans, such as giving up a day's agenda to help someone in need. To set sail on a vast uncharted sea requires the great trust of a child and the ever-willingness to sacrifice the plans of the adult personality to do instead what love demands.

To Remember

Where will love take us? No one knows, but each can say in his/her heart, "A little child shall lead me."

To Record

To Listen

No way is barred to virtue.

—Ovid

To Ponder

The task of each individual is to find a path which leads to the holy place. Regardless of the level one is at or position one is in, there is a road open to the virtuous. This is good news! The road may be steep. It may be treacherous. But no matter, a person may be down and out and full of despair, or rich, popular, and successful, but each may say, "There is a way to get there from here." Knowing this is freeing. It frees one from the feeling that he or she is unworthy of so lofty a life.

To Remember

Persist in virtue and ye shall overcome.

To Record

October 23

To Listen

No longer virtuous, no longer free.

—Benjamin Franklin

To Ponder

If we do not act on what we believe and know to be "best," we lose our freedom to choose. Much of the human organism is like a bio-computer which has been programmed to respond in certain mechanical ways to various stimuli. Most of this mechanical behavior is from our past social conditioning. What's exciting, though, is that we have a "manual override" and can choose our course of action. If as growers, we are aware of this possibility, we can operate our bio-machine and can act in any situation out of loving purpose instead of mechanical ways. To operate on manual override, however, one must be awakened to an awareness that one is a spirit who happens to have a body and mind which are to be used as instruments that serve the spirit.

To Remember

If you don't use it [your freedom], you lose it!

To Record

To Listen

Virtue conquers envy.

—Latin Proverb

To Ponder

The lack of personal right action leads to envy of right action in others. We wish we were like them, or we try to be someone other than who we truly are. This becomes doubly frustrating because we haven't been given the necessary qualities to be someone else, nor will the circumstances of life cooperate for they are wisely designed to help us develop our own qualities.

We must come to know in our heart (for it is the heart that envieth), that "It is my developmental task to become me; I will not be faulted for not becoming you."

When acting virtuously you are your true Self. In fact, it is only in those moments that you are your true Self.

To Remember

I'm OK and you're OK, thought of as a process of becoming, means I don't have to be you, nor you, me.

To Record

October 25

To Listen

All the devils respect virtue.

—Ralph Waldo Emerson

To Ponder

Virtue here is the undoing of all deceit. The devils, therefore, unleash their harshest and most subtle attacks against virtue. They respect inner strength of individuals. Strength is tempted by strength. No virtue, Immanuel Kant observed, is ever so strong that it is beyond temptation.

To Remember

"But," says Confucious, *"one whose mind is really set on virtue will do no evil."*

To Record

To Listen

Virtue withers away if it has no opposition.

—Seneca

To Ponder

Our belief system, our truths and notions of what is right and good must be challenged in order that what is integral to our virtue becomes strong while what is not really true to our highest principles fall away.

Milton said, "I cannot praise cloistered virtue that never sallies out and sees her adversary." "Cloistered virtue," virtue untested by stress and temptation of the world, is not yet ready to face the rigors of everyday living. It may be easier for a priest to remain calm during the short time he is around noisy children than for a careworn mother who has to be around them constantly.

To Remember

Without challenge there is no growth.

To Record

October 27

To Listen

Ye were not formed to live the life of brutes, but virtue to pursue, and knowledge high.

—Dante

To Ponder

One needs to become aware of one's power. Strength and authority over others expressed without self-awareness is brute power. This is depicted in mythology as the giants, stupid and insensitive. It is a potential in every person which must be overcome by intelligence and gentleness. In so doing, the energy is not lost, but transformed into that humble and wisely guided strength so necessary in the search for the highest good. For, to reach the secret place of the most holy, will require a mighty struggle. There will be "dragons" to face, boulders to remove from the path, and riddles to be solved, but those who acquire higher knowledge and apply it to the best of their ability will find the strength to scale the heights.

To Remember

May I a Jedi-warrior be.

To Record

To Listen

This alone can stand the buffets of life's battle, a just and virtuous heart, in whomso found.

—Euripides

To Ponder

Without a compass to give direction in life, the "battle" is lost. We would be buffeted about, this way and that, by life's circumstances like a ship at sea in every storm and wind. The "north star" by which we steer a true course in life is to strive to apply always the best that we know to the best of our ability. Anything else would lead us off-course. Following this star will always bring us back on course.

To Remember

No wind blows favorable to one who has no port of destination.

To Record

October 29

To Listen
Virtue never grows old.

—George Herbert

To Ponder
As a high action becomes second nature to a person, he/she must stretch to yet higher levels for it to be virtuous. Because of this, virtuous action never becomes routine. The highest good always escalates until one is ultimately acting godly.

To Remember
Growing old in the spirit is a continual process of self-renewal.

To Record

To Listen
Seek virtue, and to that possest, to Providence resign the rest.

—Benjamin Franklin

To Ponder

Seek ye first the kingdom of God and everything else will fall into place. Your personal ego has its proper responsibility in dealing with the ordinary aspects of life, but when you awaken to spiritual reality, your ego is totally lost and afraid. Ego, then, must be willing to turn responsibility over to a higher force, the divine Higher Self. The ego gets nervous about doing this and experiences free-floating anxiety. It can, however, rest assured that if the person seeks always to do the virtuous thing, Providence will take over the rest.

To Remember
Let go, and let God.

To Record

October 31

To Listen
He who dies for virtue does not perish.

—Plautus

To Ponder
Every effort one makes at being virtuous works to develop qualities of soul which are in alignment with spirit. Such gains are never lost. When the soul has brought itself into complete atunement with spirit, it will participate in the soul-spirit union for all eternity, thereby becoming immortal. This union is the "mystical marriage" spoken of so often in esoteric teachings.

To Remember
It is not just in fairy tales, for the bride and groom of this marriage will live happily ever after.

To Record

DISCERNMENT AND THE GIFTS OF THE SPIRIT

One of the most difficult passages of scripture for us to understand is the 12th Chapter of I Corinthians. Here, Paul writes about the gifts of the Spirit; at the same time, however, he admonishes his readers to be fully informed regarding their value and their practical application in the life of the community and in the world. The people to whom Paul was writing desired for themselves the extraordinary manifestations which they felt represented the presence of the Spirit. Like all of us, they often forgot that the importance does not lie in the external display but rather in how we relate and respond to those around us, as a result of the inner connection with the Spirit. The truly important aspect of the gifts of the Spirit is feeling, knowing, and experiencing spiritual peace—a gift which is invisible to the physical eye, in all but the most subtle ways.

Just as we each have different talents and ways of expressing those talents, we may also experience varieties of spiritual gifts. The same God (Spirit), however, is the author of these gifts which are only to be used in the service of selfless love to the community and not in the service of the ego self. The important point for us today is that there are still diversities of gifts, and we express these in many ways —including teaching, art, music, literature, medicine and related healing arts, etc.—even through our conversations with those close at hand.

The gifts to which the passage speaks are still manifested today in various ways. The first two—the gift of wisdom and the gift of knowledge—are not easily distinguishable. Perhaps they could be explained as the gift of stating the facts of the teachings (knowledge) and the gift of explaining the meaning of the teachings, in terms of daily spiritual living. The third gift is that of faith which in some persons is like a light shining forth in the darkness—unshakable and steadfast. The fourth and fifth gifts are healing and miracles. Healing would seem to spring forth from the working of faith and is directed toward the total person, body and mind and spiritual needs. Healing takes place through faith and prayer as the expression of those who possess the gift. The working of miracles relates to the Greek word for miracles which is the word for power and really means "the demonstration of mighty powers." Clearly faith, healing, and the working of miracles are inter-related.

The last four gifts cited seem to belong together. They are prophecy, speaking in tongues, and the ability to evaluate the prophecy and interpret the tongues. Although the gifts of interpretation may not seem as glamorous as the gifts themselves, the interpretation is essential. Symbols and ecstatic utterances may speak quite convincingly of the power of the Spirit—and may be treasured as such, but without clarity, they cannot point to the purposes of God, regarding the inner, hidden aspects of the future and the ways in which one's spiritual concerns should be guided. Thus, discernment provides clarity through keen insight and a talent for separating the wheat from the chaff.

Truly, discernment today is just as it was 2,000 years ago. It is so easy for us to get carried away by the thrill of self-display and our own self-gratification, instead of providing the service of selfless love to those around us. The admonition for us today is to remember always:

> By their fruits ye shall know them.
> Matthew 7:16

ABOUT THE AUTHOR

Paul Brecht Fenske is now serving on the Executive Committee as President-Elect of SFF. He taught on the university level in Hong Kong and served as a university minister and lecturer in the United States. At present he works with small groups and workshops in the field of spirituality and lives with his wife 'Pat' in Philadelphia.

—the Editor

To Listen

If I. . .have not love I am but a noisy gong or a clanging cymbal.

—I Corinthians 13:1

To Ponder

The 12th and 13th chapters of First Corinthians provide perhaps the clearest statement in Western spiritual literature relating to the needed perspective concerning "the gifts of the Spirit" or what many call psychic gifts or tools.

By themselves these powers are always tricky. They are very alluring. It seems they are truly primary tools of service. But service to what? They can serve ego and separation as well as Spirit and healing.

It is absolutely essential to accept, first, not the psychic gifts, but the Spiritual Treasure of Love. Love permeates our very being transforming, correcting and healing. Love is of God, channeled by Spirit and so is the prime divine trait we need for spiritual awareness and unfoldment. All other things we need will be given to us.

To Remember

If there is one thing to choose, let me choose love this day.

To Record

November 2

To Listen

So grant thy servant a thoughtful mind. . .that I may distinguish right and wrong.

—I Kings 3:9

To Ponder

Discernment is the act of distinguishing. We are constantly confronted by the making of decisions. In the world, on this plane of existence, there is a myriad of decisions to be made each day. So making decisions is our basic work.

We can make decisions at random, or we can develop somewhat more systematic ways of choosing which path to take. We can choose to act on the resultant basis of peace or pain; of love or fear, or of forgiveness or attack.

All choices are made on the basis of perception—correct or incorrect. Mistakes can be corrected so errors provide opportunities to learn and to clarify. The more we stop, observe and choose wisely, the more balance and harmony comes into our lives.

To Remember

The Spirit waits quietly to be asked to guide me as I seek to make decisions.

To Record

To Listen

The word of God is living and active, sharper than any two-edged sword...discerning the thoughts and intentions of the heart.

—Hebrews 4:12

To Ponder

Discrimination is the fine art of sorting things out. It is a gift to be able to separate the valuable from the less valuable.

In spiritual matters this has to do with what gives life the highest meaning. It is what is called happiness in the Beatitudes. Another word for it is peace. A rule of thumb that we can use to test a thought, act or feeling is, will it bring peace or pain. If it brings peace, through an inner intuitive awareness, we know it is of Spirit. If it produces uneasiness or any expression of pain we know it cannot be of God.

To Remember

May I become so discerning that my will is in accord with God's will.

To Record

November 4

To Listen

*O man, the Lord requires that you shall do jus-
tice and love mercy and be ready to walk after
him.*

—Micah 6:8

To Ponder

As we focus our hearts and minds on
thoughts of discernment these days, it is correct
to be aware of feelings, thoughts and behavior
that are inappropriate for one interested in spiritual discipline and unfoldment.

It is even more significant to keep focused on
what we need to hold in our hearts and minds
that will enable us to choose wisely and to
resonate with the will of God. The prophet
Micah, in today's thought indicates three such
guides: do what is in harmony with the spiritual
law, be quick to forgive and be compassionate,
and maintain a balanced sense of personal
worth.

Holding on to energies and experiences that
keep us in balance enables us to withstand
those forces that tend to upset, mislead and
weaken us.

To Remember

*Let me more fully balance the human and divine
aspects of my nature.*

To Record

To Listen

Blessed is the man who listens to me.

—Proverbs 8:34

To Ponder

To be discerning we must learn to listen.

These words from Proverbs speak of a great truth. Putting these words into practice helps us to live more Spirit-filled and guided lives.

Two voices speak in our lives. One voice speaks to misguide, confuse and lead us in a way that brings pain and disharmony. The other voice is the voice of God which speaks the truth and guides us to live peacefully and harmoniously so we may have lives filled with love.

To live in this way, we must learn to filter out the sounds of the "world" and listen to God's voice. It takes discipline to hear God's voice, but we will know it by the peaceful feeling it gives us as we listen.

To Remember

To follow the guidance of the Holy Spirit is the greatest step I can take.

To Record

November 6

To Listen

Choose once again.

—A Course in Miracles

To Ponder

Life is not an experience set in concrete. It is constantly moving and changing. In every moment we are making choices and decisions which will have an impact on our futures.

Every thought, feeling, decision and action is significant. We are constantly saying "yes" or "no" to being faithful to our participation in life as sons and daughters of God. It is of vital importance to know that we are not robots or puppets, but rather spiritual beings free to think, to love, to laugh and to pray.

To make choices that add to the Kingdom of Heaven indicates a significant level of discernment for administering healing love and radiating the light of the Spirit.

To Remember

Every moment presents us with a clean slate upon which we can record a new insight.

To Record

To Listen

Two roads diverged in a wood, and I—
I took the one less traveled by,
And that has made all the difference.

—Robert Frost

To Ponder

From our beginning to this very moment we all make choices. We have no alternative. Even when we make no decision we choose because there is a result.

Choices are pointers to the future. They determine direction. As Robert Frost wrote, "I took the one less traveled by." So, every path we choose leads us, in a unique way to the next point of choosing.

Choices can be threatening if we feel our role to be the victim.

But choices can be exhilarating if we see every choice leading us back to our source. If we see the universe as benevolent, then, every choice leads us back to God and the fuller experiencing of our higher potentials.

To Remember

Let me experience and express the dynamic opportunities afforded me in making wise choices.

To Record

November 8

To Listen

I choose the joy of God instead of pain.

—A Course in Miracles

To Ponder

The unfoldment of the Spirit in our lives is like the opening of a beautiful blossom. Every choice, every decision we make results in movement. The movement is either in the direction of peace or pain, love or fear. Our motivation for direction is linked to whether or not we remember who we are and what is our purpose in being here.

To move in the direction of peace is to remember we are children of God. Our mission is to live, once again, in a way appropriate to our heritage. To choose the ways of peace is to bring healing to ourselves, to our brothers and sisters and to our planet. Blessed are the peacemakers for they shall be called the children of God.

To Remember

Choose this day to become peacemakers.

To Record

To Listen

Sickness is a choice of weakness, in the mistaken conviction that it is strength.

— A Course in Miracles

To Ponder

In George Orwell's novel, 1984, he coins the term double-speak to denote that words are often used to mean just the opposite of their normal meaning, e.g., war is peace.

So it is when we say "sickness is strength." Sickness may be used to control, to get sympathy or special favors, to avoid painful situations or, ultimately, to destroy ourselves. But it never leads to strength.

To be strong in life is to know that we are sons and daughters of God. All of the power and the wisdom of the Divine is available to us for the asking. In that strength all is possible.

To Remember

Today, I choose not the weakness of sickness, but the strength of wholeness.

To Record

November 10

To Listen

No man can serve two masters.

—Matthew 6:24

To Ponder

The spiritual life is a way of power, in part because it is a way that is direct and clear. Where Spirit moves uninhibited, mighty work is accomplished: healing occurs, lives are transformed, visions are made manifest, mountains are moved.

To avail ourselves of that power it is essential for us to choose to open our hearts and minds and hand them over to be guided and taught by the Holy Spirit. Resonance with the power of Spirit will enable us, as Jesus proclaimed, to do even greater works than he had done.

To Remember

Serving two masters results in fragmentation, impotence, and confusion.

To Record

To Listen

Men can help change the course of their destiny by changing the shape of their character, intelligence, and talent.

—Paul Brunton

To Ponder

Destiny and fate are often confused. We see ourselves as pawns on a chess board being moved by the whim of some external and impersonal force. There is nothing we can do to alter the movement our lives take. This is to take a fatalistic view of life. But it has little or nothing to do with destiny.

We do have a stake in shaping our destiny. Our true destiny is implied in the words *religion* and *yoga*. The inner meaning of both of these words indicates a linking or joining back to our source, which is to God.

Our destiny is determined by our saying "yes" or "no" to the question constantly being posed by the indwelling Spirit, "Do you will to be joined to me?"

To Remember

In every moment I deeply desire to open myself and let the Spirit shape my destiny.

To Record

November 12

To Listen

The material man rejects spiritual things...
because they are spiritually discerned.

—I Corinthians 2:14

To Ponder

It is impossible to be grounded both in the material and spiritual realms. They are mutually exclusive. One of the most difficult lessons to learn is that at a given moment we can't be partly involved in spirit and partly in the world. In this moment we can only do one thing. We can only experience Spirit if we are 100% embracing Spirit.

And so the ego is hard at work convincing us that we can have it both ways. It works hard to confuse, to separate, to bring sickness and ultimately death. Naturally, it rejects things spiritual, because true devotion to things spiritual diminishes the impact and control ego has over our lives.

To Remember

Let the Spirit guide and teach me, restoring me to wholeness.

To Record

To Listen

Beware of false prophets.... You will know them by their fruits.

—Matthew 7:15–16

To Ponder

False prophets along the spiritual path are legion. The world of ego and desire offer many temptations behooving the spiritual traveler to be clear about the nature of the journey. The greatest of all false prophets is our own lower self. The philosopher Pogo aptly states, "We have met the enemy and they is us."

It is necessary to be discerning, to know the difference between the path of devotion and responsible service and the path of self gratification. One offers peace. The other pain. This is always the test. If we want peace then we must choose to follow the inner spiritual guide that leads us through the maze of life to remembering our heritage being sons and daughters of God.

To Remember

Help me to be true and faithful to that within me which knows the truth.

To Record

November 14

To Listen

You must not eat from the tree that yields knowledge of good and evil.

—Genesis 2:17

To Ponder

We human beings have eaten this fruit. Now we bear the consequences of having to make choices.

The ultimate choices we make have to do with our returning to the source from which we have come. Our first decision was to separate ourselves from God. Now, we want to make those decisions which will bring us back to a meaningful relationship with our God.

It sometimes seems to be such a difficult choice. And yet we are told that God is closer to us than the very air we breathe. It is comforting to know the One who can help us is so near at hand. And so we come full circle.

To Remember

When I am confused, I know that the Holy Spirit will give me clear guidance.

To Record

To Listen

Then Jesus was led up by the Spirit into the wilderness to be tempted.

—Matthew 4:1

To Ponder

Before Jesus began his formal ministry he went away to a wilderness area to be by himself to prepare for his task. There he went through a purification or initiation for his coming ministry.

While in the wilderness he was confronted with thoughts of acts he could do in order to gain personal power and attention. In each case he saw through the temptation. He could see what the result would be. In each case he refused to choose personal gratification, even though the temptations seemed to be acts of service.

Each day we have our challenges. We are given opportunities to sharpen our discriminatory faculties.

To Remember

In moments of temptation may I have the wisdom to turn to the Spirit for guidance.

To Record

November 16

To Listen

Seek first his kingdom and his righteousness and all these things shall be yours as well.

—Matthew 6:33

To Ponder

The key to this statement is the word *first*. If we don't take the correct first step we won't be able to take the correct second step.

Here Matthew is stating that seeking the Kingdom of Heaven is essential. Go to the place where the rule of God is active. Since Spirit resides within each of us, that is the place. Go within, seek guidance, be attentive in listening, and put into practice what comes to us in our quiet moments of listening.

Knowing this, we can then go about living in a peaceful and joyful way, aware that once we are spiritually in harmony all our needs will be supplied.

To Remember

The key to returning to our Source is going within to get directions.

To Record

To Listen

Rise and enter the city and you will be told what
you are to do.

—Acts 9:6

To Ponder

Paul was stopped abruptly by a bright light
flashing around him. Then, he heard the voice
of Jesus giving instructions for him to follow.

Paul was bent on persecuting Jesus' disciples.
That desire left him immediately when he
heard the voice of Jesus. There was no question
of what he was to do. He was stopped in his
tracks and was turned around to pursue an entirely new endeavor.

When the voice of God comes it speaks with
authority and opens up new avenues for our
lives. If we listen we will be given instructions
to go into our own cities and learn what we
must do to be faithful servants to our brothers
and sisters.

To Remember

Let us prepare to become receptive. God has
great things for us to do!

To Record

November 18

To Listen

He who is slow to anger appeases strife.

—Proverbs 15:18

To Ponder

Anger is but the tip of rage's iceberg. It is the expression of an intense desire to attack. Here we feel that our "turf" has been violated and we must protect what is rightfully ours.

When we discover that we own nothing, and that all we are and have ultimately belongs to God, there is no place for anger. When we know that, then we can share. We can give and receive, and we can lovingly communicate knowing that in this way the Kingdom of Heaven is enhanced.

The beginning of this shift is to observe the feelings of unrest we have—examine these, see their potential for bringing anger—then, decide for peace instead, dismissing the unrest as undesirable.

To Remember

I truly want to be at peace.

To Record

To Listen

Where there is no vision the people perish.
> —Proverbs 29:18

To Ponder

Vision, in one sense, implies a looking ahead, not absolutely certain of the outcome, but having an intense willingness to move ahead toward the Imaged goal.

Those with no vision lack enthusiasm and purpose. They lust after unspiritual stagnation and seek the "easiest" way through life. Their idea is to be cautious and reduce the level of risk. Their motto might well be, "nothing attempted, nothing done."

Every gifted inventor or explorer—every person on a spiritual quest has a vision. Vision implies resoluteness and facing squarely ahead with elevated sight. To accept a vision and pursue it leads us into the realm of the mystical where meaningful and fulfilling spiritual experiences are to be encountered. These lead us on to a devotion to faithful service.

To Remember

May I live the vision that all minds are joined and all hearts are one.

To Record

To Listen

Be as wise as serpents and as harmless as doves.
—Matthew 10:16

To Ponder

Here we find one of the best descriptions of a truly spiritual person. In esoteric literature the serpent is representative of wisdom, the dove of peace.

The wise person sees clearly, is not taken in by the attractions of the "world," and draws conclusions which lead to healing of peace. To harmonize the inner knowing of wisdom with the inner feeling of peace is to arrive at a point of balance and centering which we all seek in our spiritual questing. Spiritual knowing and feeling enables us to love fully and unconditionally.

The spiritual path is a gentle way that neither judges or harms anyone. To be at that point of balance is the perfect place from which to make decisions and begin to act.

To Remember

Wisdom and gentleness provide an optimum environment for discernment.

To Record

To Listen

After the fire a still small voice...
—I Kings 19:12

To Ponder

The greatest illusion, perhaps even blasphemy, is to believe we are isolated, alone and apart. That is a false idea from our lower selves and not the reality of the matter.

No matter where we are, the still small voice of God is with us to give us companionship, guidance and counsel. One of the most precious promises of God is that we are not alone. Jesus said he would leave a comforter with us when he physically departed from the earth. That still small voice is ever with us to remind us who we are. God is the beloved one who not only reminds us of our identity, but invites us to act on that identity becoming co-creators as the Sons and Daughters of God.

To Remember

Hear the voice of God, then express the light of God in my life.

To Record

November 22

To Listen

Forgiveness offers everything I want.

—A Course in Miracles

To Ponder

We want to be free. We want to be happy. We want to give and receive love.

The only barrier to our having these things is that we also want to hold on to experiences from our past which cause us pain and make us fearful. When we get to a point where we are sick and tired of being sick and tired, then there is hope for a change.

By asking Spirit to help, we are able to let go of the past and live this moment with a fresh and unbiased perspective. By forgiving, we are able to choose love instead of fear and so bring balance and harmony into our lives and the lives of those about us.

To Remember

Let me learn from the past and let it go.

To Record

To Listen

The promises of God are absolute!

—Annalee Skarin

To Ponder

One evening several years ago I was reading from Annalee Skarin's book, *Beyond Mortal Boundaries*. The above statement was repeated several times. All of a sudden from deep within my consciousness a sense of profound affirmation came into my conscious mind, "Of course it is true!!!" God's promises are true. The Bible and other spiritual literature is filled with these ideas.

When we come upon them there can be no doubt—only affirmation. In them there is coherence; they are a direct and clear link to Spirit. In them there is resonance; they reverberate throughout the universe in harmony with all Divine principles.

This is the way of Divine discernment. It fills us with *absolute certainty* that we are Beings of Spirit, here to manifest Spirit.

To Remember

I come from Spirit;
I am filled with Spirit;
I will manifest Spirit.

To Record

November 24

To Listen
One person and God is a majority.

—Allen Wehrli

To Ponder
The greatest tragedy of human history is that we misunderstand who we are. We are taught that we are either puny, miserable creatures totally incapable of doing anything worthwhile or else that we are all-powerful and self-sufficient beings who are complete masters of our fate. Both have elements of truth and misinformation.

We are never self-sufficient. But when we align ourselves with the power and presence of God, all that God is is available to us. Those who are faithful to that inner beckoning of God find themselves infused with unlimited dynamism. All truly great people—creative people, saints, masters, teachers, prophets and servers of humanity—are aware of the great spiritual potential which they draw on for sustenance and guidance.

To Remember
I give thanks for the mystery and for the remembrance of who I AM.

To Record

To Listen

Nor do they light a lamp and put it under a bushel, but on a stand.

—Matthew 5:15

To Ponder

The Light shines within each of us for we are the dwelling places of the Holy Spirit. Our life mission is to recall this reality.

But it is not enough to know the Light is within. We have come to earth as servers. Our calling is to stand aside, let Spirit shine through our lives, and thereby to reach out and trigger the illuminating of light in the lives of others.

And so we join together with kindred souls to let the light of peace, joy, love, and truth flood over and transform the quality of life that is manifest on Planet Earth.

To Remember

We are light bearers. We ask to be guided in assuming and carrying out that role.

To Record

November 26

To Listen

The real miracle is not to walk either on water or in thin air, but to walk on earth.

—Nhat Hanh

To Ponder

Life is filled with the unexpected.

It is easy to be attracted to the spectacular. But we live in that realm only in rare moments.

The lessons of life take place in the day to day realm. If we live well through the experiences of this day, we will indeed live well.

The goal of life is to live each moment to its fullest potential. To do so means we will have no regret of past actions and no fear of the future. To walk on the earth treasuring each moment enables us to sense beauty, to know joy, to be filled with peace, to give ourselves in service and to express love unconditionally. Then, if we experience serendipitous events, we will be lifted to ecstasy.

To Remember

Expressing our divinity is more important than to wait a lifetime for the unusual to emerge.

To Record

To Listen

I can find a beautiful place;
Or I can make a place beautiful.

—Author Unknown

To Ponder

It is easy to wish, to idly hope or to lament and blame. To take any of these attitudes is to hand over our responsibility. We can spend a lifetime looking for the right place or the best thing.

By continuing to look for meaning in places, people or things outside ourselves we will miss what is truly the most beautiful—the awareness and the unfoldment of spiritual beauty within our own lives.

When we begin to find the inner beauty, a profound miracle begins to take place. We become increasingly aware that the more beauty we find within, the more beautiful other things appear.

To Remember

I will spend some time today discovering the beauty that lives within my self.

To Record

November 28

To Listen

The more faithfully you listen to the voice within you, the better you will hear what is sounding outside.

—Dag Hammarskjold

To Ponder

Our experiences from the past have taught us to be suspicious and apprehensive, because the world in which we live seems to be unreliable and hostile. In that environment it is easy to sense that we are vulnerable and victims.

To be trapped by such thinking is unnecessary. Once we become aware of our true nature as spiritual beings, we understand the source of our strength and protection comes from the Spirit which dwells within each of us. Nothing can harm us once we become aware of this reality.

We become invulnerable and invincible to the external forces which issue frightening sounds from outside ourselves. And once we are aware of the indwelling spirit, those sounds lose their fearsomeness.

To Remember

I trust in Spirit's love.
I no longer fear dark dwelling "demons."
I am at peace.

To Record

To Listen

With knowing comes responsibility;
With responsibility comes choice;
With choice comes the future.

—Author unknown

To Ponder

We have within us the seed of knowing for we
are created in the image and likeness of God—
the all knowing One. That knowing is as near to
us as seeking, knocking or asking. More is
revealed to us as we use what we have. That is
being responsible.

The more responsible we are the more choices
are given to us. The laws of the cosmos are
orderly. We are given exactly what we are
capable of handling. If we want a fuller
experience, we choose to respond to more of
the challenges that are offered to us.

The goal of life is to help shape the future in
such a way that love is extended so that all of
humankind might be One and the Kingdom of
Heaven be fully manifest in the Earth.

To Remember

*I have the ability to respond to the divine
Knower as I choose my future.*

To Record

November 30

To Listen

I want the peace of God.

—A Course in Miracles

To Ponder

I can either be happy or right. It is easy to claim to be right. Such claims are often hollow because they leave us feeling cut off from or in opposition to some one else. So what has been gained.

If we think and act in such a way as to bring happiness and blessings into our lives and the lives of those about us, we truly make a contribution. We need not claim anything. We are and do those things which bring balance, healing and oneness.

These acts are motivated by the stuff of Spirit. Unlike being right everyone can join in seeking after the true happiness which Spirit in action can bring.

To Remember

Let me not seek to be right, but to seek the highest good for all.

To Record

UNITY AND ONENESS

In a sense everything we do hinges on the reality of the unity and oneness of all in the universe. When we accept this realization, it releases us, and we soon find that life takes on a new meaning and a new order. Isolation is not possible, in this reality, and neither is aloneness for we are never truly isolated or alone. Nature and everyone and everything in the universe is woven together into one tapestry.

Sometimes we get caught in thinking of our body, or our skin as our "encapsulated self" and separate. We look at reality as if, "I am in here, and the world is out there." We forget that what we do about the inner self, we also do about the world. I and everybody and everything else, at their most fundamental level, are of one essence. A difference exists, however, between experiencing the awareness of unity and oneness and conceiving of it with our minds.

At the very moment we perceive ourselves and experience the world as a single whole, the assurance of the oneness is ours, never to be lost again during this life time. Such a moment may come through the beauty of the sunset in nature, through meditation, through intense emotion, through the music of the African drums or through visions of Earth and space blending together. When we have this awareness, then unity becomes for us the fundamental basis of all our perception, thinking and action. We can no longer return to the dualistic "skin model." Unity and oneness mean coming together as a whole, but they do not necessarily mean uniformity. Diversity always exists, but a concern for the well being of all must also inform our reality. This concern consists of an overriding compassion in which love, harmony, peace and justice for all reign supreme. When we see a common thread running through all of humanity, every breath we take expresses the interconnectedness we feel; yet, even in the awareness of that likeness, we sense as well our own external, unique configuration—a composition of cells, atoms and photons, not to be seen ever again. In this sense, our unity lies in the strength of our diversity.

No thing is separate from any other thing in the universe. The auric fields, often invisible to our eyes, are all woven together. With everything which happens, we can "feel" ourselves moving toward a deeper sense of this awareness. Often in the stillness, we intuitively feel and know that the *interconnectedness* and *oneness* we share relates back to a common ancestry. We are of the family of creation, unbegun and unending; we are the essence of life, cousin to the star and the tigress. From the swirl of motion at the dawn of this phase of existence, the spark of all being ignited the universe. Down the long evolution through time and space, the eternal fire has given us kinship. This is the primordial memory, the spiritual bond we may forget but never break. We each must call ourselves to continue to remember and experience the injunction:

> *There is one body, and one Spirit...*
> *of us all, who is above all, and through*
> *all, and in all.*

> Ephesians 4:4-6

ABOUT THE AUTHOR

Elizabeth Wall Fenske is currently completing her sixth year as President of SFF. For the past thirteen years, she has been on Executive Council, and she has spoken, led workshops, and traveled widely representing SFF in the United States and abroad. She has a private practice in psychotherapy, is listed in a number of biographical reference works (Who's Who in the East, etc.), and lives in Philadelphia with her husband, Paul.

—the Editor

To Listen

The path is one for all, the means to reach the goal must vary with the pilgrims.

—The Tibetan Doctrine

To Ponder

The pilgrim, it has been said, is the person who passes through life as if in exile from a heavenly homeland. The pilgrim may be in search of the homeland, or of some higher goal, such as truth. Some pilgrims may be quite clear about their destination, and may take direct means while others may be more uncertain and less focused in their pursuit. Deep within each pilgrim, however, is the longing to return home.

No matter what course is taken, only one destination exists—the path to attain the goal. We, with our various interpretations and varieties of religious and spiritual beliefs and insights, are *all* on the same pilgrimage. The *path* for *all* humankind is the same one.

To Remember

No one goes somewhere new; we all return to the same homeland.

To Record

December 2

To Listen

The one is none other than the all, the all none other than the one.

—Seng Ts'an

To Ponder

Throughout time there has been, on the mental level of consciousness, the question of the two powers of Good and Evil. All evils, however, represent temporal powers. The only eternal power is God. Evil is a suggestion, a temptation we do not have to accept. We can turn to our spiritual heritage and accept the *ONE* God (energy) as the *ALL*.

The Augustinian interpretation of the fall of Adam and Eve as Original Sin caused in the Judeo-Christian heritage a misinterpretation of the spiritual nature of humanity. Since energy of the *ONE* is not evil, there are no evil persons, although at times evil may manifest in our actions. Thus, our spiritual destiny is that ONE and ALL are equal.

To Remember

There is no separation of the one from the all or all from the one.

To Record

To Listen

From of old the things that have acquired unity are these: Heaven... Earth... The Spirit... The Valley... All things by unity have come into existence.

—The Tao-Te-King

To Ponder

The Chinese, down through the ages, have always seen life as being in harmony with nature and the universe. This passage leads us to recognize that the Chinese also understood the secret of manifestation and the unifying energy, force or power behind the existence of all that is. They perceived that the heavens were clear, the earth was steady, the Spirit was the author of spirituality and the Valley possessed a fullness.

The Heaven represents air; the earth is earth. Spirit is Fire, and Water resides in the Valleys. Thus, the four elements cause all things to come into existence.

To Remember

The author of all that is is unity.

To Record

December 4

To Listen

Receive the word of wisdom that opens all things and come to know the hidden unity in the Eternal Being.

—Evelyn Underhill

To Ponder

The direction for mystics has always been toward the presence of the Light which illuminates and unifies them with the Eternal Ground of all Existence and Beingness. Thus, one of the experiences of the many who follow the mystic way is "To know the hidden unity in the Eternal Being."

Many have felt that the life of the mystic involves removing oneself from the life of the world. Evelyn Underhill, one of the greatest mystical writers of the Twentieth Century, points out, however, that living at the fullest the illuminated life means enjoying, "all creatures in God and God in all creatures." Thus, the Hidden Unity in the Eternal Being is that all things are joined together into oneness.

To Remember

The Light which illuminates is the light of oneness.

To Record

To Listen

God and man (woman) are ONE, just as the glass and the tumbler are one.

—Joel Goldsmith

To Ponder

The very essence of the tumbler is glass. When the glass is shaped, however, and blown into a tumbler, it possesses a different form of beauty. It is more than just a piece of glass; yet, its essence is glass. It exists for a certain purpose.

God is more than us; yet, our essence is of God. God is the substance of our life, of our body, mind and soul. A person is the Temple, the form, just as the tumbler is the form of the glass. God is the essence of each person just as the glass is the essence of the tumbler.

To Remember

The glass can not be separated from the tumbler, nor can God be separated from man (woman).

To Record

December 6

To Listen

One in all,
All in one.
If only this is realized
No more worry about your not being perfect.

—Buddhist Scripture

To Ponder

One of the secrets of spiritual healing is our attunement to the energy within the universe and each other. When we share a healing experience with another person, attunement becomes real for us. In the stillness, while silently sensing a common flow of energy, there is the realization of "one in all, all in one." There we know that we are each truly *ONE* part of the *ALL* and that the *ALL* is within each *ONE* of us.

This *ALL* in each *ONE* of us is also *ONE* with *ALL* of us. Therefore, we each share our imperfections as well as sharing our perfections. Thus, responsibility for more spiritual living is on all of our shoulders alike.

To Remember

All for one, and one for all.—Dumas

To Record

To Listen

I am in you and you in me,
mutual in love . . .
Fibers of love from man to man . . .
Lo! we are ONE

—William Blake

To Ponder

A real possibility exists that what the great poet William Blake was telling us is the same thing we are on the verge of understanding through our current exploration in Modern Physics. Today also, Psychic Research is seeking both to quantify the nature of energy and to prove the community of this energy (fibers) to everything within the universe, including all of humankind. This energy is within each of us individually and all of us collectively at the same time. It finds its expression in LOVE, and it is this LOVE which is the FIBER THAT CONNECTS each of us together in a oneness. When we fail to recognize this oneness, we are denying ourselves LOVE. When we express this oneness by showing forth LOVE to each other, we fulfill our joint divinity and oneness.

To Remember

Love knits the fibers in each of us together into one tapestry.

To Record

December 8

To Listen

The basic oneness of the universe is not only the central characteristic of the mystical experience, but...one of the...important revelations of modern physics.

—Fritjof Capra

To Ponder

C. G. Jung introduced us to the term synchronicity, a concept which deals with the acausal connections of symbolic images which may manifest themselves in both the inner psychic world and the events of the external world of reality. For Jung, these synchronistic happenings were expressions of the "acausal orderedness" in mind and matter.

Today in modern particle physics, there is a talk of ordered connectedness. Even though distinctions can be made between the kinds of connections, patterns of mind and patterns of matter seem to reflect one another. One way to explore the relationship between the inner and outer realms is to study the order in causal and acausal connectedness. It seems clear that situations are experienced simultaneously by the conscious as well as the unconscious aspects of our Being.

To Remember

Innate order within our being is in touch with innate order outside our being.

To Record

To Listen

...*That they may all be one; even as thou,
Father, art in me, and I in thee, that they also
may be in us...*

—John 17:21 (RSV)

To Ponder

This particular passage in John's Gospel has
been known as Jesus' Prayer for the Unity of
the Church Universal. The hope was that in the
future, after the apostolic preaching, there
would be Unity in God and a shared fellowship
like unto that which Jesus had with God, the
Father. This unity comes as a gift of divine love,
but it demands a unity of individuals.

If people recognize, acknowledge, and draw
close to the unity they have in and with God,
the Father (one Spirit in the Universe), then
automatically the flow which follows is toward
union with one another. To come together in a
Spirit beyond our individual differences makes
for a healthy environment for the presence of
love.

To Remember

The universe is one, and we are one with it!

To Record

December 10

To Listen

I and all things in the universe are one.

—Chuang-Tzu

To Ponder

The Chinese speak of the Tao, being the Eternal Way, and they seek to live life in the flow of this Way. Part of this is the recognition of the connection they have with everything in the Universe. They not only connect, however, they literally *feel themselves* as part of the whole, the ONE, total whole.

For the Chinese, Tai Chi is the way of being a part of and moving harmoniously with the Universe. Their brush strokes in calligraphy portray the same harmonious movement. So does the bamboo and the peach blossom—two of the symbols which they paint. They believe they are one with the heaven and the earth, the yin and the yang forming for them the Tao, the Way.

To Remember

To be in harmony is to be one with the universe.

To Record

To Listen

No man is an island, entire of itself; every man is a piece of the continent, a part of the main.

—John Donne

To Ponder

We have all heard either the words or the song "No man is an island!" Truly today, no one is an isolated island unto themselves. Everyone is, however, a piece of the continent. We are each involved in all of life. We are all receptive, whether we recognize it or not, to the charts of the stars as well as to the charts of our own physical anatomy. Both are involved in our destiny and we in theirs, in a peculiar way.

Just as there is no separate individual, in the truest sense of the word, there is no absolute individuality. It is by the Grace of the Universe that we live, and as its name implies, it is truly ONE. The deepest longing within all of us is to be reunited with the main, the continent of the whole.

To Remember

Life guides us down the living stream that leads from the Island to the continent(s).

To Record

December 12

To Listen

Eager to maintain the unity of the Spirit in the bond of peace

—Ephesians 4:3 (RSV)

To Ponder

Only two places in the New Testament use the word unity. One is in the quotation cited above, and the other comes from the same chapter, in verse 13 where the writer speaks of the unity of the faith. This does not refer to an inward unity as opposed to an external unity. It is referring to the unity which the spirit of Christ consciousness creates.

Deeply rooted in the Old Testament is the conviction of the unity of God, which in Deuteronomy 6:4 is recorded, "Hear, O Israel, the Lord our God is one Lord." This creed was recited by every Jew, and the early Christians took it for granted. Today both Judaism and Christianity face disunity for they have lost and fragmented the inward connection to the Unity of the Spirit.

To Remember

We are all one celebrated people, who have received one law from ONE.—Apocalypse of Baruch.

To Record

To Listen

There is but one religion; the many faiths and creeds are all streams or steamlets of this great river.... The Sun of Truth is One.

—G. R. S. Mead

To Ponder

The root word of religion literally means to bind back, to yoke or tie back to the source. The source of the existence of all that is, is one; thus, we all are in the process of returning to our original source of being. This has been true since the beginning of all time, and humanity has, with its diversity of cultures, languages and experiences, expressed these ideas about its spiritual nature in many different ways. So we have today many faiths, creeds and religions.

We must think of the source of our existence as being likened to a great river which branches off into many streams which likewise break off into many streamlets and tributaries. Yet, the source is ONE. This is likened unto the SUN of truth being ONE.

To Remember

From the one comes the many to express and return once again to the ONE.

To Record

December 14

To Listen

All the cosmic patterns, the secrets of the Universe, are embedded in our muscles and bones and cells, in... the context of the self.
—George Leonard

To Ponder

The reality of this statement finds its truth in an analogy to the concept of the hologram. In the hologram a fragment of a picture contains all of the picture when a laser beam of light passes through the fragment. It is as if the cosmic patterns and secrets of the universe are waiting for us to shine the light of consciousness onto them.

Our greatest dilemma at unveiling these truths and secrets lies in the conscious reality of our living in the presence of seeming opposites. We know these secrets are a part of divine heritage; yet, we fear them on the human plane. The Divine and human planes of life are not competing opposites, rather they are complementary of each other.

To Remember

The photons of the self mirror and reflect the photons of the cosmos.

To Record

To Listen
When we try to pick out anything by itself we find it hitched to everything else in the universe.
— John Muir

To Ponder
There are behind this thought a myriad of explanations, and that, in itself, is what the sentence is all about. Within our unconscious, there is housed everything which has ever happened to us. Our interconnectedness with each other and with others is also there. Buried in my unconscious are my experiences with those of you who read these words and vice versa. If we were to pick one thought from our unconscious, and trace it backward, we would find that the thought is connected to many others.

The thought is connected to the brain, the brain to the head and spine, blood supply, nerves, tissues and ultimately to the body. The body is connected to the environment, the earth, and ultimately to the Universe.

To Remember
Eveything is ultimately one, with no inner or outer barriers.

To Record

December 16

To Listen

All that man has . . . is intrinsically ONE. Here all blades of grass, wood, and stone, all things are ONE. This is the deepest depth.

—Meister Eckhart

To Ponder

The great mystic Meister Eckhart expresses for us, through his poetic words, the universal truth of unity and oneness. He felt that those things which we see in multiplicity in the external world really are intrinsically one. It matters not the actual composition or make up of that of which we speak. It may be stone or wood, or even a blade of grass. Still they are all interconnected and one.

The connection is not on the external level, for here we see in shapes and forms and perceive things to be different. It is on the inner level, which lies in the deepest depth visible only to our inner perception, where the common energy flows and make the connection. Here all things are ONE.

To Remember

When we FEEL our oneness with another, we SEE less separateness.

To Record

To Listen

ONE radiant energy pervades and gives rise to all life.... All (plants, nature spirits or humans) are reflections of the deeper reality within.
—The Findhorn Garden

To Ponder

Behind all of life is the same creative energy which moves the stars and planets in the sky and causes the earth and moon to orbit the sun. This same energy gives life to the plants, nature spirits, and humans. This energy is deep within everything which exists. It is the vibration, the rhythm of the universe or universes.

In Northern Scotland, near the shores of the North Sea at Findhorn, lie the Findhorn Gardens the special charm and beauty of which many have traveled miles and miles to see. These gardens are truly reflections of the one Energy that is ever-present there and everywhere. Each time we tune in to the deeper reality within, the life energy residing there answers us. It is only a thoughtform away.

To Remember

So is God the nature, essence... unto every form, including man, animals, plants and minerals.
—Joel Goldsmith

To Record

December 18

To Listen

All living creatures reflect the same universal intelligence and can communicate with each other when they make contact on the same level.

—Paul and Blanche Leonard

To Ponder

We all know what it is like to tune the radio gently to the proper channel to make contact with vibratory waves of energy. The clue is in stabilizing the level for proper communication.

Living creatures reflect, possibly from the universe, levels of intellect by which they can communicate with each other when they are on the same frequency. The experimental work of Cleve Baxter of San Diego, California shows us that this communication can also take place with plants and animals.

Our gray, short-haired tabby cat used to come into the house from the backyard when we sent him the thought to come in because we were going out. Thus, we were somehow able to touch in with him on the same frequency level.

To Remember

There is one infinite Intelligence moving through all life.—J. Allan Boone

To Record

To Listen

*Who sees all beings in his own self and his own
self in all beings, loses all fear.*

—The Upanishads

To Ponder

One of the deepest fears is the fear of confrontation with our fellow humans. We become fearful of another and withdraw into our own little cocoon. Yet life has a way of mirroring to us what we really look like, and most of the time there are many similarities in the expressions of our humanness.

When we are able to see our own self in others, then we can more closely observe others in our own self. When this happens, our reward is that we begin to lose our fear of not being accepted, and soon we find the secret lies in first accepting ourselves, then accepting others. Thus, we achieve a sense of calm through knowing our Unity with each other.

To Remember

*Joy is ours; we know in unity that the SELF and
all beings are one.*

To Record

December 20

To Listen

All forms of life with which man comes in contact are eligible for this communication in a grand ONENESS.

—J. Allan Boone

To Ponder

In his book, *The Kinship of All of Life*, Allan Boone explains that the possibility exists for us to communicate with all forms of life. His profound sense of oneness led him to experience an exchange with a common domestic housefly whom he knew in a personalized way as *Freddie!* Although this type of communication takes a great deal of time and patience, it is very rewarding for we then feel that spark of energy which binds everything into oneness. To communicate we must first desire the experience; then we must send out the thought that we will do no harm to the life form, and finally, we must open ourselves for the communication to be returned to us.

To Remember

A thought sent in a true spirit of love comes back to enrich our lives.

To Record

To Listen

At every step along the way, every entity is connected to the great web of information that is the universe.

—Bradford Smith

To Ponder

In reality none of us is ever *alone* for we are a part of all that is. It is as if the universe in which we live and move and have our Being is one gigantic communcations system, which contains information about all that exists. Through attuning ourselves to this *web of information* with each step we take, we keep our connection open, if we but listen and respond.

When the spider builds a web, each thread is connected to another. Each of us is also connected, like threads, to every other person and to the universe. We often miss the signals given to us because we seek to go our separate ways; yet, the connection always remains.

To Remember

To think the thought of our connectedness is to bring it into being.

To Record

December 22

To Listen

We are united with all life that is in nature. Man can no longer live his life for himself alone.

—Albert Schweitzer

To Ponder

Many people of the world know of the life and work of Albert Schweitzer and his deep sensitivity to and reverence for life. He excluded NO THING from his consciousness. As long as we ignore our unity with all life that is a part of nature, we are prone to live as if we alone were the center of creation. But when we see, sense and feel life pulsating in all that is around us, we are no longer able to isolate or idealize only our own existence. Schweitzer was one who not only heard the music of nature, both earthly and heavenly, but who was able to play this music upon the organ. Likewise, we need each day to take a cue from him and unite ourselves more fully with all the life in nature.

To Remember

Music is a universal language of heaven and earth, spoken to us through nature.

To Record

To Listen

All things by immortal power, Near or far, Hiddenly to each other linked are, That thou canst not stir a flower without troubling a star.

—Francis Thompson

To Ponder

The connection which links all things together is the immortal power of divine energy. Whether these things are close by or far away, they are nonetheless joined in a subtle relationship which is hidden from outward observation. In Francis Thompson's verse, we have portrayed for us one of the greatest contrasts between near and far—the flower which is in reach and the star which is almost inconceivable in its distance. Yet the connection is surely there; each time we touch a flower, the stars feel the vibration.

It has been said that a child cannot throw a toy from the play pen without the stars knowing it. We are only fooling ourselves when we think that what we do affects only ourselves.

To Remember

Perfect freedom is the handmaiden of total responsibility, for nothing escapes being linked to everything.

To Record

December 24

To Listen

On every act the balance of the whole depends. . . . We must learn to keep the balance.
— Ursula LeGuin

To Ponder

One of the greatest challenges we all face today is to find and maintain balance in our own lives, in our communities, countries and the Universe. Nothing is without its counterpart to bring about balance, which is always changing and even redefining its space. Each time there is movement, the balance changes and the whole must be jockeyed into another position.

This means we must become sensitive to the balance in all of life and always seek to be aware of the consequence of all our actions. We each affect the whole. To learn to keep the balance is a part of the process of living life to its fullest so that we fulfill our responsibility to the balance of the whole, for ourselves and everyone else.

To Remember

The counterpoint of balance is deep within our inner being.

To Record

To Listen

Behold, how good and pleasant it is when brothers dwell in unity.

—Psalm 133:1 (RSV)

To Ponder

In Biblical times, when this psalm was written, there were two important interpretations of brothers dwelling together in unity. The nation of Israel was thought of as a community where people dwelt together in unity as brothers dwell together. Second, often several generations or brothers of families lived together. Also when the families separated through travel, they would come back together at given times. It was good and enjoyable when the families were once again united together.

One of the ways we can manifest in our daily living the reality of our unity and oneness is to walk in humility and spiritual awareness with the words on our lips that it is "good and pleasant...when we dwell together in unity."

To Remember

If we can learn to live together in peace and unity, how different things will be.

To Record

December 26

To Listen

The wonderful telepathic communication throughout the universe is such that in the ONE Cosmic Mind there is no distance and no separation.

—Paul Brunton

To Ponder

The great Western mystic, the late Paul Brunton knew what it meant to be in tune with the ONE Cosmic Mind. In his book, *Inner Reality,* he points out to us that the first step of mysticism is for each person to touch into the soul *within* and find the Father's Spirit dwelling there. The second step is to touch into the universe and see and know that there is also that same Spirit dwelling everywhere.

And this Spirit dwelling everywhere is the One Cosmic Mind which everyone is capable of communicating with by means of telepathic thought processes. It transcends all boundaries, and in it there is no separation or distance from the Spirit. Just as the Spirit within us is joined to the Spirit in the Universe, so today all minds are joined together.

To Remember

He who has once seen his real self will never again hate another.—Paul Brunton

To Record

To Listen

Because we shirk the practice of oneness we are prisoned in self and cut off from the replenishing springs of life.

—Bradford Smith

To Ponder

To be concerned only about our own self sets us apart from the natural expression of the oneness of us all. This causes us to be caught in our own world and isolated from those around us. It is as if we are locked into a prison, and the key is lost for we feel lost.

Under the earth, there are ever-flowing springs, which are connected to the streams, inlets and tributaries. Often the life of the spring depends on those flowing into its body of water. Nature has a way of practicing its ONENESS naturally, and all functions in harmony. So too must we function in order to replenish our life with the ONE life force.

To Remember

Oneness is our birthright and the birthright of all who accept it.

To Record

December 28

To Listen

When you lose contact with nature, you lose contact with every human being.

—Krishnamurti

To Ponder

On the higher levels of consciousness there is no distinction between the outer and the inner for there is no space or time, but all space and all time. We are prone to think in terms of spirit and matter as separate entities whereas, in essence, spirit (energy) is all there is. The way in which energy collects gives us visual differences we call matter.

The human is the replica of the universe of nature. The Arcane teaching "as above, so below" uses the expression "we are the microcosm and the macrocosm"—what is outside is within. If we, in our technological advancements come to the point of cutting ourselves off from nature, we will come to the point of cutting ourselves off from each other.

To Remember

Nature is the life which connects us to our life!

To Record

To Listen

The spiritual workers have to redeem the world...by bringing home to it the truth of the UNITY OF ALL LIFE.

—Meher Baba

To Ponder

In his *Discourses*, Volume III, Meher Baba points out that the soul sometimes identifies itself with its various bodies or its ego-mind of the mental body. The bodies all become "mediums," he says, for experiencing different states of the world's duality. The soul of each person often touches into these various states of consciousness.

God is the reality and unity of all souls. This unity is the bond which joins all souls to the Universal Soul of God. This then brings the bodies into a unified whole. As each part of our body becomes unified, our life is unified. The task of the Spiritual worker is to be about verifying, by example, this unity of all the life within our bodies.

To Remember

By unifying our oneness within our living, we reflect the unity of all life.

To Record

December 30

To Listen

At the heart of each of us, whatever our imperfections...exists a silent pulse of perfect rhythm...which connects us to everything in the universe.

—George Leonard

To Ponder

Within each of us there is that spark of perfection which will always remain and can not be extinguished by another. This spark has been called by many names throughout history. It is, as George Leonard says, *a silent pulse of perfect rhythm*, and it draws all of us together and connects us to each and every thing that exists within the universe. It does not matter how much we fall short, the *silent pulse* is always ready to welcome us home and to stabilize our existence.

When we stay in touch with this silent pulse and connect with the rhythm of the universe, transforming personal experiences always await us. Look this day to touch into this perfect rhythm.

To Remember

The perfect rhythm within the universe transcends all our imperfections.

To Record

To Listen

Change breaks down our boundaries, links us to all else, providing the grounds of our interconnectedness, our interdependency.

—Thomas Buckley

To Ponder

One of the most constant things in the Universe is change. Yet, it is often very difficult for us to feel we are changing, or that we are affecting change. We must never underestimate the importance of developing the ability to desire and accept change in our lives.

When we embrace flexibility, we find that change comes more naturally; we do not have to fear impermanence, and the reality of interdependency becomes our gift. The more barriers we destroy, the closer we come to each other; and the closer we come to each other, the more we all feel our interconnectedness. As we approach the New Year—a time of change, will we acknowledge the power and potential of change in our lives?

To Remember

Even though we may not perceive a change, everything is constantly changing.

To Record

AFTERWORD

It has truly been a joy to share with you, through the pages of this small book, as you have traveled this year on your spiritual pilgrimage. The thoughts and words presented have not necessarily been new thoughts; they are as old as the power of thinking and have taken many literary forms in the past. The messages—whether they come to us from the pens of mystics, scholars, religious figures, prophets or peasants, no matter if they are 30,000 years old, or as contemporary as today—all have a sacredness for us and a ring of familiarity. Hopefully, these words have helped us each to find our own words from within our Inner Sanctuary.

The Spiritual Insights we are each seeking to glean are those truths which have passed the test of time, which are *eternal*, and which belong to all of humankind. These truths are closer to us than the air we breathe, in fact they are in the very vibrations of the breath which pulsates within us. These truths know no boundaries, no limitations and are as true for the infinite life of the universe(s) as they are for us in our own daily living. These vibrations of the truths and insights of the words are mirrored in both nature and humanity. In our travels through life, we must be about uncovering the treasures along our paths.

As we have *listened* in the stillness, *pondered* by the Light, *Remembered* from the past and *Recorded* for safe keeping, we have harvested from the storehouses of our inner temples great nourishment for our souls. Here at this most authentic holy of holies we have found eternal challenges. Yet, we have also realized once again that both the inner and the outer realities are woven tightly together, never to be separated, for they actually find that the only reason for their existence lies in the joy of their interdependence. And so commitment finds its rightful place in our unfoldment in consciousness.

We open ourselves anew to the love all around us as we accept the roles we each must play in our world—a world where many do not yet know the liberation of responsible freedom, yet carry on their daily work. We realize that as their hearts ache, so do ours. We hear their cries; we taste their bitterness and touch into the space occupied by their fears—fears for their security and for that of their children and their children's children.

As you have turned these pages you have, no doubt, been aware of the number of themes which have reoccurred in all the months, no matter what the particular subject may have been. This always seems to be true for us! For truth comes dressed in many garments and spoken through many different sources. We must each take it where we find it, wrap its mantle about us and listen to its echos. We must trust the admonition to "*know thyself,*" for it is in *knowing ourselves* that we return to the *point of Light* when we "*experience thy Spirit.*" It is there then that we truly *know* that life is for living on both the *human* and *Divine* planes at the same moment, within space and outside space.

This little book, like our lives, began as an open book in which we could fill the blank spaces with words. Yet, truly, we need no words, for words will not complete the book's message. Its message can only be completed within our hearts. We must not let it exclude another similar book from our consciousness; instead, we must be open to other readings which will come to us because we've shared *these* pages. If you choose, you may travel through its pages again next year and discover anew what esoteric gems the exoteric words crystalize in your consciousness.

May we each, in his or her own way, ignite more brightly the *Inner Lights,* as we continue to travel separately, yet together on our spiritual pilgrimage.

—the Editor

SPIRITUAL INSIGHTS FOR DAILY LIVING:
A Daybook of Reflections on Ancient Spiritual Truths of Relevance for our Contemporary Lives...

This publication of Spiritual Frontiers Fellowship was edited by Elizabeth W. Fenske. If you would be interested in purchasing additional copies of this book, or in receiving information about SFF, please fill out and send the order form below to:

Spiritual Frontiers Fellowship
3310 Baring Street
Philadelphia, PA 19104.

☐ Please send me _____ copies of ***SPIRITUAL INSIGHTS FOR DAILY LIVING*** at $7.50 per copy. My check or money order, in the amount of _____, in U.S. dollars only, is enclosed.

☐ Please send me more information about Spiritual Frontiers Fellowship.

Name _____

Address _____

City _____ State _____ Zip _____

Country _____ Date _____

To Record

To Record

To Record